I0439796

July 2014

# COASTAL ZONE MANAGEMENT

## Opportunities Exist for NOAA to Enhance Its Use of Performance Information

GAO-14-592

## COASTAL ZONE MANAGEMENT

## Opportunities Exist for NOAA to Enhance Its Use of Performance Information

# GAO Highlights

Highlights of GAO-14-592, a report to congressional committees

## Why GAO Did This Study

The U.S. coast is home to more than half the U.S. population and integral to the nation's economy. Under the Coastal Zone Management Act, NOAA administers the CZMP, a federal-state partnership that encourages states to balance development with protection of coastal zones in exchange for federal financial assistance and other incentives. In 2008, GAO reviewed the CZMP and recommended improvements for CZMP performance assessment tools.

A fiscal year 2013 appropriations committee report mandated GAO to review NOAA's implementation of the act. This report examines (1) how states allocated CZMP funds awarded in fiscal years 2008 through 2013 and (2) how NOAA's primary performance assessment tools have changed since GAO's 2008 report and the extent to which NOAA uses performance information in managing the CZMP. GAO reviewed laws, guidance, and performance-related reports; analyzed CZMP funding data for fiscal years 2008-2013; and interviewed NOAA officials and a nongeneralizeable sample of officials from seven states selected for receiving the most fiscal year 2012 funding in each of NOAA's regions.

## What GAO Recommends

GAO recommends that NOAA document an approach to analyze and revise, as appropriate, its performance measures against key attributes, revise its process for selecting stakeholders to survey in its state program evaluations, and document a strategy for using the performance information it collects. NOAA concurred with the recommendations.

View GAO-14-592. For more information, contact Anne-Marie Fennell at (202) 512-3841 or fennella@gao.gov.

## What GAO Found

During fiscal years 2008 through 2013, the 34 states participating in the National Oceanic and Atmospheric Administration's (NOAA) National Coastal Zone Management Program (CZMP) allocated nearly $400 million in CZMP funds for a variety of activities. States allocated this funding for activities spanning six broad focus areas based on goals outlined in the Coastal Zone Management Act. For example, states allocated about a quarter of their CZMP funding to the coastal habitat focus area, according to NOAA's analysis. Coastal habitat activities encompassed a variety of actions to protect, restore, or enhance coastal habitat areas, such as habitat mapping or restoration planning efforts of marsh habitats for fish and wildlife and enhanced recreational opportunities.

NOAA's two primary performance assessment tools—its CZMP performance measurement system and state program evaluations—have limitations, even with changes NOAA made since 2008, and NOAA makes limited use of the performance information it collects. Regarding the performance measurement system, NOAA has made changes such as taking steps intended to improve the reliability of data it collects. However, its current measurement system does not align with some key attributes of successful performance measures, including the following:

- *Balance: a balanced set of measures ensures that a program's various goals are covered.* NOAA removed the coastal water quality focus area, one of six focus areas based on goals in the act, to streamline the performance measurement system. As a result, the system may not provide a complete picture of states' overall performance across all focus areas based on goals in the act.
- *Limited overlap: measures should produce new information beyond what is provided by other data sources.* NOAA's system includes measures that overlap with financial data provided in cooperative agreements. By requiring states to submit financial data available through other sources, NOAA may be unnecessarily burdening states with data collection requirements.

NOAA plans to review and potentially revise its measurement system, but it has not documented the approach it plans to take, including how the measures will align with key attributes of successful performance measures. Regarding state program evaluations, in 2013, NOAA revised its process to conduct evaluations more efficiently, at a reduced cost. However, GAO identified a limitation in NOAA's method for sampling stakeholders to survey under its revised process that may result in the selection of stakeholders that do not span all six focus areas based on goals of the act. Finally, NOAA makes limited use of the performance information it collects from these tools. For example, since it began collecting performance measurement data in 2008, NOAA used the data once to report on accomplishments. NOAA recognizes the importance of using performance information to improve program implementation, but it has not documented a strategy for how it will use its performance information to manage the program. As a result, NOAA may not be realizing the full benefit of collecting performance information.

# Contents

Figures

**Abbreviations**

| | |
|---|---|
| CZMP | National Coastal Zone Management Program |
| EPA | Environmental Protection Agency |
| GPRA | Government Performance and Results Act of 1993 |
| NOAA | National Oceanic and Atmospheric Administration |
| OCRM | Office of Ocean and Coastal Resource Management |

# GAO

U.S. GOVERNMENT ACCOUNTABILITY OFFICE

**441 G St. N.W.**
**Washington, DC 20548**

July 16, 2014

The Honorable Barbara Mikulski
Chairwoman
The Honorable Richard Shelby
Ranking Member
Subcommittee on Commerce, Justice,
Science and Related Agencies
Committee on Appropriations
United States Senate

The Honorable Frank Wolf
Chairman
The Honorable Chaka Fattah
Ranking Member
Subcommittee on Commerce, Justice,
Science and Related Agencies
Committee on Appropriations
House of Representatives

The U.S. coastal zone—which includes areas along the Atlantic, Pacific, and Arctic oceans, the Gulf of Mexico, and the Great Lakes—is home to more than half of the population of the United States and plays an integral role in our nation's economy, contributing to over half of the U.S. gross domestic product and supporting more than 66 million jobs. The coastal zone provides harbors for ports, shipping, and navigation; opportunities for energy production from traditional sources such as offshore oil, and alternative sources, including wind, tidal, and wave; beaches and shorelines for recreation and tourism; and wetlands and estuaries that are critical for sustained fisheries. The coastal zone also provides important environmental benefits including filtering pollution from runoff; buffering shoreline communities against storms; and providing habitat including spawning grounds, shelter, and food for marine life, and other threatened, endangered, and commercially important species. Increased population density and economic activity in the coastal zone, however, puts pressure on coastal habitats.

In 1972, Congress enacted the Coastal Zone Management Act to balance the often competing demands for economic growth and development with the need to protect coastal resources.[1] In doing so, Congress recognized that states have primary responsibility for planning and managing their coastal zones. On this basis and to help achieve the goals of the act, the Department of Commerce's National Oceanic and Atmospheric Administration (NOAA), which has responsibility for implementing the act, administers a voluntary, cooperative program established under the act known as the National Coastal Zone Management Program (CZMP).[2] The CZMP involves federal and state partnerships that encourage coastal states, Great Lakes states, and U.S. territories and commonwealths[3]—hereafter referred to as states—to balance and manage economic development and coastal protection. To participate, states must develop and implement a comprehensive coastal management program that addresses specific goals established in the act and meets other federal requirements, but states have the flexibility to design programs that best meet their own coastal needs. NOAA provides funding and technical assistance to support administrative and project-specific costs for state coastal management programs (state programs) it approves to participate in the CZMP. In fiscal year 2013, 34 of 35 eligible states had state programs and received CZMP funding.

NOAA evaluates the CZMP's performance using two primary tools—its CZMP performance measurement system and state program evaluations. NOAA, working with state programs, developed the performance measurement system in the mid-2000s, in response to congressional direction to assess the national impact of the CZMP and report on progress in meeting the act's goals. In addition, NOAA is required under the act to conduct evaluations of each state program to assess its adherence to the act's requirements. NOAA also collects performance-related information from other sources, such as semiannual progress

---

[1]Pub. L. No. 92-583, 86 Stat. 1280 (1972) (codified as amended at 16 U.S.C. §§ 1451-1466).

[2]Other programs established under the act and administered by NOAA include the National Estuarine Research Reserve System—a network of protected areas that provide research, education, and resource stewardship to help communities address coastal resource issues—and the Coastal and Estuarine Land Conservation Program, a funding program which provides matching funds to state and local governments to purchase priority coastal and estuarine lands of ecological, conservation, recreational, and historical importance. These programs are outside the scope of this review.

[3]For purposes of the CZMP, the term "coastal state" is defined to include Puerto Rico, the Virgin Islands, Guam, the Northern Mariana Islands, and American Samoa.

reports submitted by participating states describing progress in implementing their cooperative agreements. Cooperative agreements are the mechanisms by which NOAA provides congressionally appropriated financial assistance annually to states for the program activities they have agreed to undertake under the CZMP. We reviewed the CZMP in 2008 and made several recommendations to address weaknesses we found in NOAA's use of its tools to assess the performance of the CZMP, among others.[4] NOAA agreed with all but one of our recommendations, and it has taken steps to address the majority of our recommendations.

The House Appropriations Committee report for the Department of Commerce Fiscal Year 2013 appropriation mandated us to examine NOAA's implementation of the Coastal Zone Management Act.[5] Focusing on CZMP activities since our 2008 report, this report examines (1) how participating states allocated CZMP funds awarded in fiscal years 2008 through 2013 and (2) how NOAA's primary performance assessment tools have changed and the extent to which NOAA uses performance information to help manage the CZMP.

To conduct our work, we reviewed applicable laws, regulations, and NOAA guidance, including guidance on its CZMP performance measurement system and state program evaluations. We analyzed NOAA data on financial assistance awards for fiscal years 2008 through 2013, NOAA analyses of states' allocations of CZMP funds, and its performance measurement system data. To assess the reliability of these data, we interviewed NOAA officials and reviewed related documentation, and we determined the data we used to be sufficiently reliable for our purposes. We interviewed NOAA officials responsible for administering

---

[4]GAO, *Coastal Zone Management: Measuring Program's Effectiveness Continues to Be a Challenge*, GAO-08-1045 (Washington D.C.: Sept. 12, 2008). This report included seven recommendations—six recommendations to NOAA related to improving its assessment of the effectiveness of the CZMP and one recommendation related to improving its funding award practices. The report also included one matter for Congressional consideration that Congress may wish to clarify whether it would like eligible states to receive equal amounts of CZMP administrative funding or whether these funds should be proportional and reflect each state's respective shoreline miles and coastal population. Congress has not passed legislation related to this matter.

[5]H.R. Rep. No. 112-463, at 21-22 (2012); see also the Explanatory Statement for the Senate Substitute Continuing Resolution, associated with the Consolidated and Further Continuing Appropriations Act of 2013, Pub. L. No. 113-6, and the House report incorporated by reference. 159 Cong. Rec. S1287-01 at S1300 (Mar. 11, 2013).

the CZMP and conducting state program evaluations about the approaches they use to assess program performance, how they use performance information, and any changes they have made since 2008, including steps taken to address recommendations in our 2008 report. We also reviewed our and others' work on performance assessment, including our work on key attributes of successful performance measurement systems and elements of strong evaluation designs. We examined NOAA's publicly available reports and documents on CZMP performance, including program fact sheets, program reports, and state program evaluation results. We interviewed state program officials from the seven states that received the most fiscal year 2012 CZMP funding in each of NOAA's seven regions. These include California, Florida, Hawaii, Maine, Michigan, Texas, and Virginia. We obtained information about states' use of CZMP funds, their perspectives on NOAA's performance assessment tools, and how the results of a select project in each state we reviewed were reported to NOAA.[6] We selected projects considering such factors as amount of CZMP funding, types of financial assistance and projects, and goals established in the act. We also conducted two site visits to observe and learn more about CZMP projects—one to a coastal habitat restoration project in Texas, and one to an ocean planning project in Virginia. We selected these projects for site visits considering project type, goals of the act the project addressed, and geographic location. Appendix I presents a more detailed description of our objectives, scope, and methodology.

We conducted this performance audit from June 2013 to July 2014 in accordance with generally accepted government auditing standards. Those standards require that we plan and perform the audit to obtain sufficient, appropriate evidence to provide a reasonable basis for our findings and conclusions based on our audit objectives. We believe that the evidence obtained provides a reasonable basis for our findings and conclusions based on our audit objectives.

## Background

Congress enacted the Coastal Zone Management Act in 1972 to balance the often competing demands for economic growth and development with the need to protect coastal resources. To accomplish the goals of the act, Congress established a framework for a voluntary federal and state

---

[6]Our review of the states' information cannot be generalized across all states or projects.

coastal management partnership, the CZMP. The CZMP represents a unique federal-state partnership for protecting, restoring, and responsibly developing the nation's coastal communities and resources, according to program documents.

The act identifies specific goals for state programs that fall into six broad focus areas ranging from protecting and restoring coastal habitat to assisting with coastal community development efforts and improving government coordination and decision making (see table 1).

**Table 1: Focus Areas Based on Goals for State Coastal Management Programs Outlined in the Coastal Zone Management Act**

| Focus area | Goal |
|---|---|
| Coastal habitat | • Protecting natural resources, including wetlands, floodplains, estuaries, beaches, dunes, barrier islands, coral reefs, and fish and wildlife and their habitat, within the coastal zone |
| Coastal water quality | • Managing coastal development to improve, safeguard, and restore the quality of coastal waters, and to protect natural resources and existing uses of these waters |
| Public access | • Providing for public access to the coast for recreation |
| Coastal hazards | • Managing coastal development to minimize the loss of life and property by improper development in coastal hazard areas and by the destruction of natural protective features<br>• Studying and developing, in any case in which the Secretary considers to be appropriate, plans for addressing the adverse effects of land subsidence and sea-level rise |
| Coastal community development | • Assisting in redevelopment of deteriorating urban waterfronts and ports, and sensitive preservation and restoration of historic, cultural, and esthetic coastal features<br>• Providing for priority consideration for coastal-dependent uses and orderly processes for siting major facilities related to national defense, energy, fisheries development, recreation, ports and transportation and the location, to the maximum extent practicable, of new commercial and industrial development in or adjacent to areas where such development already exists |
| Government coordination | • Coordination and simplification of procedures in order to ensure expedited governmental decision making for the management of coastal resources<br>• Continued consultation and coordination with, and the giving of adequate consideration to the views of, affected federal agencies<br>• Giving timely and effective notification of, and opportunities for public and local government participation in, coastal management decision making<br>• Assistance to support comprehensive planning, conservation, and management for living marine resources, and improved coordination between state and federal coastal zone management agencies and state and wildlife agencies |

Source: GAO analysis of Coastal Zone Management Act.| GAO-14-592

States must submit comprehensive descriptions of their coastal management programs—which must be approved by the states' governors—to NOAA for review and approval. As specified in the act, states must meet the following requirements to receive NOAA's approval for their state programs, among others:

- designate coastal zone boundaries that will be subject to state management;
- define what constitutes permissible land and water uses in coastal zones;
- propose an organizational structure for implementing the state program, including the responsibilities of and relationships among local, state, regional, and interstate agencies; and
- demonstrate sufficient legal authorities to carry out the objectives and policies of the state program, including the means by which a state will regulate land and water uses, control development, and resolve conflicts among competing activities in coastal zones to ensure their wise use.

The act provides states the flexibility to design programs that best address states' unique coastal challenges, laws, and regulations, and participating states have taken various approaches to developing and carrying out their programs. For instance, there are generally two organizational structures used by states to implement their programs: (1) networked programs, which rely on multiple state and local agencies to implement their programs, and (2) non-networked, or comprehensive state programs that administer all aspects of the program through a single centralized agency. The coastal management activities carried out also vary across states with some states focusing on permitting, mitigation, and enforcement activities, while other states focus on providing technical and financial assistance to local governments and nonprofits for local coastal protection and management projects. If states make changes to their programs, such as changes in their coastal zone boundaries or organizational structures, the states must submit those changes to NOAA for review and approval.

The act includes two primary incentives to encourage states to develop coastal management programs and participate in the CZMP. First, participating states are eligible to receive federal funding from NOAA to support the implementation and management of their programs, which the agency receives annually through congressional appropriations. In fiscal year 2013, NOAA awarded participating states a total of approximately $61.3 million, a 9 percent decline from fiscal year 2008 awards, when it awarded just over $67.5 million across participating states.[7] NOAA awards CZMP funding to individual states across three fund types—administrative, enhancement, and coastal nonpoint program—according to requirements in the act (see table 2). The majority of funding NOAA awards through the CZMP is administrative funding. Administrative funding, which requires state matching funds, supports general implementation of the state's coastal management program. Under the act, NOAA may also award a maximum of $10 million annually in enhancement program funding to participating states. Enhancement funding is to be used by states to develop program changes, or enhancements, to their NOAA-approved programs in one or more of nine enhancement objectives specified in the act, as listed in table 2. In addition, Congress has generally provided direction on the total amount of funds to be awarded through the coastal nonpoint program to assist with states' coastal nonpoint pollution control programs, which are programs to ensure states have necessary tools and enforceable authorities to prevent and control polluted runoff in coastal areas. According to NOAA officials, funding has not been provided for this program since fiscal year 2009, when nearly $3.4 million was awarded to states. States may also use other sources of funding for their coastal nonpoint pollution control programs, including administrative and enhancement funding.

---

[7]Adjusting for inflation, the amount of CZMP funding declined by 16 percent over the 6-year period. NOAA officials noted that fiscal year 2013 levels were lower than they might otherwise be due to the across the board sequester that cut federal funding that year.

**Table 2: Types of Funding Awarded to State Coastal Management Programs under the Coastal Zone Management Act**

| Qualifications and requirements | Funding uses | Funding distribution |
|---|---|---|
| **Administrative funding (awarded through sections 306 and 306A of the act)** | | |
| • Approved state coastal management program<br>• State matching funds required | Funding is to support implementation of state programs, including<br>• personnel costs, equipment, and supplies;<br>• nonconstruction related activities such as permitting, planning, and public education type projects; and<br>• funding to others, including local governments and nonprofit organizations.<br><br>A portion of the funds may also be used for low-cost construction projects or land acquisition projects that enhance public access to the coast, facilitate redevelopment of urban waterfronts or ports, or preserve and restore coastal habitat. | NOAA determines the amount of federal appropriated National Coastal Zone Management Program (CZMP) funds to be awarded to each participating state through this funding type by<br>1. establishing a minimum and maximum award amount for states, and<br>2. applying a weighted formula that considers each state's coastal population and miles of shoreline.<br><br>Maximum administrative award a state can receive annually has generally been capped in appropriations acts at $2 million. |
| **Enhancement funding (awarded through section 309 of the act)** | | |
| • Approved state coastal management program<br>• Approved 5-year assessment and strategy report that identifies a state's priority coastal management needs and planned projects to address one or more of nine enhancement objectives<br>• No state matching funds required | Funding must be used to address one or more of the following nine enhancement objectives specified in the act:<br>1. wetland protection, restoration and enhancement;<br>2. reducing and managing development in coastal hazard areas;<br>3. increased public access to the coast;<br>4. reduction of marine debris along the coast;<br>5. control of cumulative and secondary impacts of development;<br>6. planning for the use of ocean and Great Lakes resources;<br>7. special area management planning and implementation;<br>8. facilitating the siting of energy and government facilities and related activities; and<br>9. facilitating siting of aquaculture facilities. | NOAA determines the amount of federal appropriated CZMP funds to be awarded to each qualifying state through this funding type.<br><br>NOAA's process for distributing enhancement funds to qualifying states uses a weighted formula that considers state's coastal population and miles of shoreline.<br><br>A small portion is competitively awarded through NOAA' Projects of Special Merit Program, whereby states with 5-year assessment and strategy reports submit applications for innovative projects that further enhance strategies related to select national enhancement priority areas identified by NOAA. |

| Qualifications and requirements | Funding uses | Funding distribution |
|---|---|---|
| **Coastal nonpoint program funding (awarded through section 310 of the act)[a]** | | |
| • Approved state coastal management program<br>• State coastal nonpoint pollution control program, required as part of the 1990 reauthorization of the act to further state program efforts in addressing coastal water quality protection and restoration goals, whereby states develop a program to prevent or reduce nonpoint source pollution from a range of sources[b]<br>• State matching funds required | Funding must be used to implement state coastal nonpoint source pollution control programs. | NOAA determines the amount of Congressionally directed CZMP funds to be awarded to each qualifying state through this funding type.<br><br>Amount of funds awarded to individual states considers status of coastal nonpoint pollution control program approval. States with fully approved programs received greater amounts of funding while states with conditionally approved programs, meeting partial requirements, receive less. |

Source: GAO analysis of the Coastal Zone Management Act.| GAO-14-592

[a]Section 6217 of the Coastal Zone Act Reauthorization Amendments of 1990 amended the act to require state programs to develop coastal nonpoint pollution control programs to restore and protect coastal waters. Pub. L. No. 101-508, tit. VI, subtit. C, § 6217, 104 Stat. 1388, 1388-314 (1990) (codified as amended at 16 U.S.C. § 1455b). For fiscal years 2008 through 2013, NOAA awarded funding for the coastal nonpoint program through section 310 of the Coastal Zone Management Act.

[b]NOAA and the U.S. Environmental Protection Agency (EPA) jointly administer the coastal nonpoint program at the federal level, and both agencies must approve state coastal nonpoint pollution control programs. Nonpoint source pollution is runoff from sources such as lawns, roadways, farms, construction sites, and leaking septic tanks.

Second, federal agency activities in or affecting the uses or resources of a participating state's defined coastal zone are required to be consistent to the maximum extent practicable with enforceable policies of the state's program. Under this provision, known as federal consistency, states with approved programs must have the opportunity to review proposed federal actions for consistency with enforceable policies of their state programs. Types of federal actions that may be reviewed by states include federal agency activities, such as improvements made to a military base; licenses or permits to nonfederal applicants; financial assistance to state and local governments; and outer continental shelf activities, such as oil and gas development. If a state finds that a federal activity is not consistent with the state's enforceable policies, the state can object to the activity and work with the federal agency to resolve any differences between the proposed activity and state policies. All participating state programs have developed federal consistency review processes.

Thirty-four out of 35 eligible states have federally approved coastal management programs (see fig. 1). Most state programs have been in existence for more than 30 years, with the earliest program approved in 1976, and 29 states having received federal approval for their programs by 1986. The most recent state to begin participating in the program is Illinois, which received federal approval in January 2012.

**Figure 1: Coastal States Participating in the National Coastal Zone Management Program**

Coastal and Great Lakes states and territories participating in the Coastal Zone Management Program

Coastal state not participating in the Coastal Zone Management Program. Alaska is the only eligible state not participating.[a]

Sources: National Oceanic and Atmospheric Administration; Map Resources (map). | GAO-14-592

Note: For purposes of the CZMP, the term "coastal state" is defined to include Puerto Rico, the Virgin Islands, Guam, the Northern Mariana Islands, and American Samoa.

GAO-14-592 Coastal Zone Management

aBy operation of Alaska State law, the federally approved Alaska Coastal Management Program expired on July 1, 2011, resulting in the state's withdrawal from participation in the CZMP. See 76 Fed. Reg. 39857 (July 7, 2011). Alaska participated in the program from 1979 through July 2011.

NOAA's Office of Ocean and Coastal Resource Management (OCRM) is responsible for general administration and oversight of the CZMP. NOAA plans to merge the OCRM with its Coastal Services Center—an office that provides coastal-related mapping tools and data; training on various coastal management issues such as climate adaptation and coastal restoration design and evaluation; and technical and other assistance to local, state, and regional coastal organizations—into a single office by the end of 2014. Under the current and planned office structure, NOAA officials are responsible for approving state programs and any program changes, administering federal funding to the states, providing technical assistance to states such as on the development of 5-year assessment and strategy reports that identify states' priority needs and projects to address one or more of nine enhancement objectives required for enhancement funding, among other topics, and managing the CZMP performance measurement system. NOAA assigns coastal management specialists to work with individual state programs. As part of its administration of the program, NOAA evaluates program performance using its CZMP performance measurement system. NOAA began developing a framework for this performance measurement system in 2001, started piloting it in 2004, and fully implemented the system by 2008. The system consists of 15 performance measures that generally correspond with the goals of the act, and two additional measures to track state financial expenditures. The 17 total performance measures incorporate individual data elements, plus additional subcategories of information that state programs collect and report into the system annually (see app. II).

In addition, NOAA evaluators, who are in a different NOAA division than specialists, are responsible for conducting individual state program evaluations, which are required under the act. State program evaluations are designed to examine the extent to which states have: (1) implemented their approved programs,(2) addressed coastal management needs identified in the act, and (3) adhered to the terms of CZMP funds awarded through cooperative agreements. NOAA's state program evaluation reports identify state accomplishments and make recommendations for improving states' programs. NOAA's recommendations are classified as either necessary actions—actions a state must take by a specific date such as the next regularly scheduled evaluation—or program suggestions—actions it believes a state should take to improve its program. NOAA may withdraw approval for a state's program and financial assistance in cases where states do not address necessary actions. NOAA has not withdrawn approval for a state program as of the end of fiscal year 2013 and, according to NOAA officials, few necessary actions have been identified in past state evaluations.

In 2008, we examined NOAA's process for awarding financial assistance to states and how the agency evaluated the effectiveness of the CZMP. Of the seven recommendations we made in 2008, NOAA disagreed with one recommendation that the agency develop performance measures to evaluate the effectiveness of state programs in improving processes; NOAA agreed with the other six recommendations and has taken some actions to address them as described in table 3.

**Table 3: National Oceanic and Atmospheric Administration Actions to Address Recommendations for the National Coastal Zone Management Program (CZMP) Made by GAO in 2008**

| Area for improvement | Recommendation | Actions taken | Status |
|---|---|---|---|
| Process for awarding federal funding | Review and revise, as needed, NOAA's regulations and funding award practices to ensure that they are in alignment | Fiscal year 2011 – NOAA adjusted its formula for distributing federal funding to states in accordance with its regulations.<br><br>Fiscal year 2012 – NOAA began competitively awarding funding to selected projects through its Projects of Special Merit Program, whereby states submit applications for innovative projects that further enhance strategies related to select national enhancement priority areas identified by NOAA. | ● |
| CZMP performance measurement system | Develop appropriate internal controls for verifying that the data received for the performance measurement system are reliable and consistent across participating states | April 2010 – NOAA updated its national performance measurement system guidance for states that included documentation requirements for state submitted data.<br><br>July 2010 – NOAA issued guidance to NOAA specialists on data review steps and initiated a formal review and approval process for state submitted data. | ● |
| | Develop performance measures to assess state programs' effectiveness in improving processes[a] | No action taken.[a] | ○ |
| | Create targets for existing performance measures to assess the effectiveness of the national program | Fiscal year 2011 - NOAA identified targets for several of the CZMP performance measures that NOAA and Commerce use to track progress on NOAA-specific and Commerce-wide goals related to environmental stewardship.[b] | ◒ |

| Area for improvement | Recommendation | Actions taken | Status |
|---|---|---|---|
| Evaluations of state coastal management programs | Ensure that state evaluations are independent by revising the role of state program officials in the review process | June 2009 – NOAA began to reserve time during stakeholder interviews, conducted as part of the state program evaluations, for discussion without the presence of state program officials. In the past state program officials fully participated in stakeholder interviews which we found potentially hindered open discussion about the state program. | ● |
| | Establish performance goals so that evaluators have criteria for evaluating state coastal programs | Fiscal year 2011- NOAA required state programs to develop and track annual progress on three state evaluation metrics with state established targets. | ● |
| Integration of performance assessment tools | Develop an approach to integrate the qualitative data from its periodic state program evaluations with the quantitative data in its performance measurement system | January 2013 - NOAA issued fact sheets to communicate the accomplishments of the CZMP using 2008 to 2011 national performance measurement system data and success stories reported by state programs, based on recommendations of a performance measurement system workgroup they assembled. | ◕ |

Legend:

● = Recommendation closed - implemented

◕ = Recommendation open - steps taken

○ = Recommendation closed - not implemented

Source: GAO analysis of National Oceanic and Atmospheric Administration information. | GAO-14-592

[a]NOAA disagreed with this recommendation, explaining that, after considering several process measures, it chose to include one measure related to the federal consistency process to demonstrate national program effectiveness in improving decision making. NOAA stated that additional process measures would increase implementation costs and diminish the focus on program outcomes. We believed the single federal consistency process measure did not adequately assess other key aspects of states' effectiveness in coordinating and expediting government decision making.

[b]Annual targets for one CZMP measure related to acres of coastal habitat protected were established and tracked at the NOAA and Commerce-wide levels since fiscal year 2006.

# States Allocated Nearly $400 Million in CZMP Funds during Fiscal Years 2008 through 2013 for a Wide Range of Coastal Management Activities

During fiscal years 2008 through 2013, the 34 participating states allocated a total of nearly $400 million in CZMP funds for a variety of activities, generally related to the broad goals for state programs outlined in the Coastal Zone Management Act. Each year, NOAA analyzes its cooperative agreements with states for CZMP funding, and categorizes the states' CZMP funding allocations as they correspond with the six focus areas based on the broad goals in the act, along with a seventh category to capture state program administrative costs, such as general program operations, supplies, and rent. According to NOAA's analysis, during fiscal years 2008 through 2013, states' allocations of CZMP funds varied across the seven categories, with about half concentrated in support of activities related to two focus areas, government coordination and coastal habitat (see fig. 2).

**Figure 2: States' Coastal Zone Management Program Funding Allocations by Focus Area, Fiscal Years 2008 through 2013**

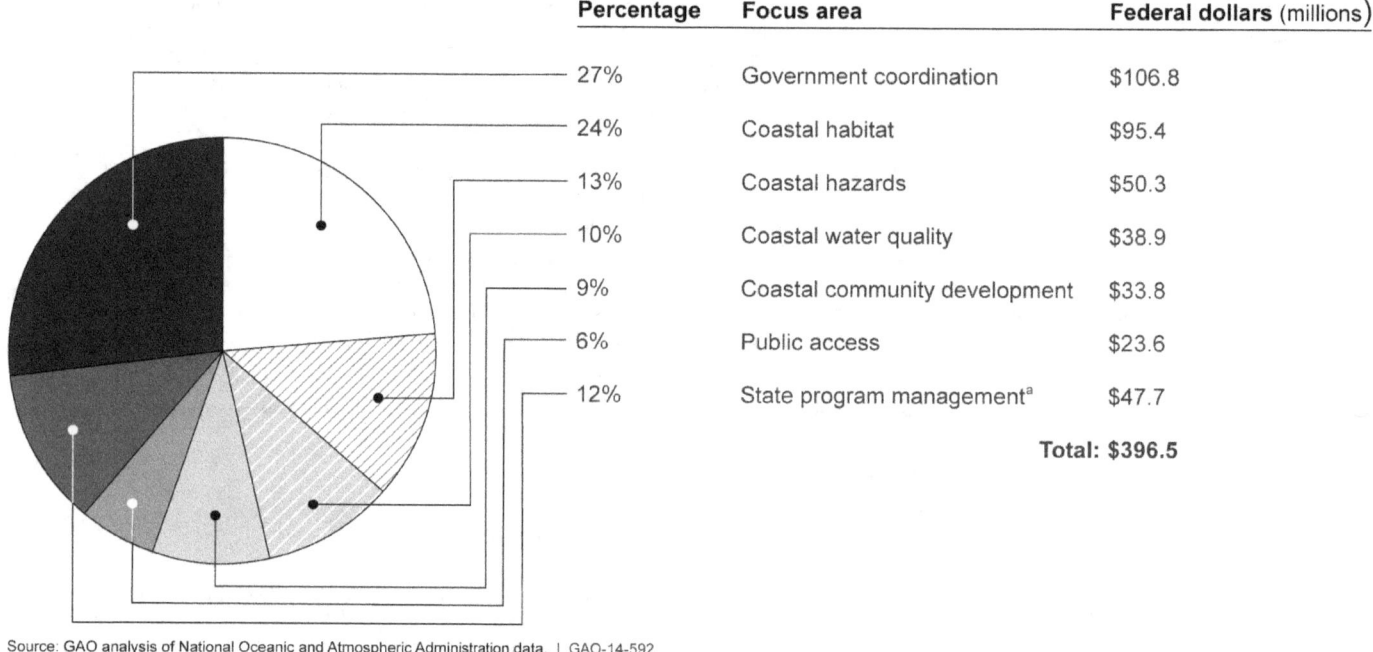

| Percentage | Focus area | Federal dollars (millions) |
|---|---|---|
| 27% | Government coordination | $106.8 |
| 24% | Coastal habitat | $95.4 |
| 13% | Coastal hazards | $50.3 |
| 10% | Coastal water quality | $38.9 |
| 9% | Coastal community development | $33.8 |
| 6% | Public access | $23.6 |
| 12% | State program management[a] | $47.7 |
| | **Total:** | **$396.5** |

Source: GAO analysis of National Oceanic and Atmospheric Administration data. | GAO-14-592

Notes: Percentages do not add to 100 percent due to rounding.

Focus areas and the state program management category are defined by NOAA, and amounts are approximate. CZMP funded activities could address more than one focus area. To address this challenge, NOAA developed written guidance for NOAA specialists who conduct the analysis that specifies the types of activities to include in each focus area and the state program management category, and direction on how to categorize funds in cases where a project or activity may fall in more than one category.

[a]State program management is not a focus area, but rather it is a category used by NOAA to track CZMP funding not directly associated with the six focus areas, including state program administrative costs, such as general program operations, supplies, and rent.

NOAA officials told us that, while states have the flexibility to design and implement programs that best meet their unique needs, the agency does influence how states allocate CZMP funds through (1) NOAA's review and approval of states' 5-year assessment and strategy reports required for enhancement funding in which participating states prioritize projects that support program improvements and (2) NOAA's periodic state program evaluations in which NOAA outlines necessary actions or makes program suggestions that can influence state program activities. NOAA officials said that they also informally shape or influence state program

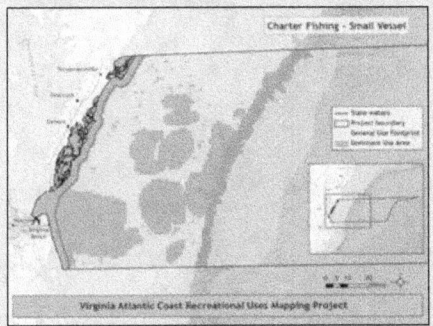

activities through ongoing discussions with state program officials about funding proposals or specific projects, such as how projects might be adjusted to address NOAA priorities.

Examples of activities for which participating states allocated CZMP funds during fiscal years 2008 through 2013 in each of the six focus areas include the following:

- **Government coordination.** States allocated CZMP funds for activities including state and regional planning efforts that involve coordination among multiple levels of government and stakeholders to address complex and controversial coastal issues, such as comprehensive planning of ocean and nearshore areas, energy facility siting or special area management planning;[8] federal consistency activities;[9] technical assistance to local governments; and public outreach and education on coastal issues including website development and publications about a state program's activities. According to NOAA's analysis of cooperative agreements with states for CZMP funding, states allocated the largest amount of CZMP funding during the 6-year period—about 27 percent of total funding—to government coordination activities. We found that a number of state programs use CZMP funds to support participation in regional organizations involving ocean planning activities that entail coordination across federal, state, and local governments. For example, state program officials in some Northeast and Mid-Atlantic states participate in regional organizations, such as the Northeast Regional Ocean Council and Mid-Atlantic Regional Council on the Ocean, that have ocean resource data collection and planning efforts under way. We also found that most states we reviewed provide some

---

[8]Special area management plans are one of nine enhancement objectives eligible for enhancement funds. The act defines a special area management plan as "a comprehensive plan providing for natural resource protection and reasonable coastal-dependent economic growth." States have used such plans to address complex coastal issues, such as waterfront revitalization, in discrete geographic areas.

[9]Under the federal consistency provision of the Coastal Zone Management Act, federal agency activities affecting any land or water use or natural resource of a participating state's defined coastal zone are required to be consistent with enforceable policies of the state's coastal management program to the maximum extent practicable. State federal consistency reviews involve states' assessments of proposed federal actions that include federal agency activities, licenses or permits to nonfederal applicants, financial assistance to state and local governments, and outer continental shelf activities to ensure consistency with state program policies.

The Texas state program used coastal zone funds to support a multiyear marsh restoration project on the Texas Gulf Coast near Corpus Christi. Over the past 60 years, about 340 acres of coastal marsh habitat were lost due to the construction of an adjacent highway and subsequent erosion. A local nonprofit organization began restoring the marsh in 2005. The project involved scooping sand, clay, and shells from the bay bottom and piling the material into terraces and mounds; planting native grasses on the terraces to stabilize the structures and provide habitat; and constructing an outer rock berm to protect the new marsh area from strong waves in the bay, as shown below.

Project officials told us Texas's state program provided about $1 million in coastal zone funding, about 20 percent of the project's total cost, to the nonprofit organization responsible for the project. Other funding to carry out the project was provided by the EPA, U.S. Fish and Wildlife Service, state government sources, and grants from private foundations. According to project officials, the project was completed in spring 2014 and has resulted in 160 acres of restored marsh that provide habitat for fish, crabs, shrimp, nesting birds, sea grass, and other plants and animals. The project also resulted in the creation of new opportunities for public recreation, such as fishing and kayaking, and the marsh protects the adjacent highway from coastal hazards, such as storms, according to project officials.

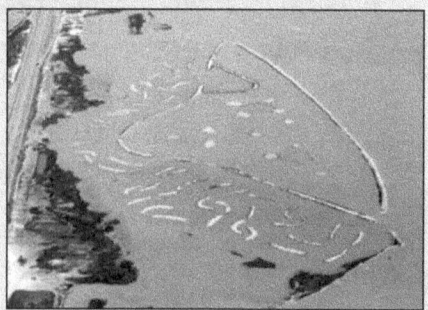

Earthen terraces and mounds provide restored marsh habitat along the Texas Gulf Coast.

Source: Lanmon Aerial Photography, Inc. | GAO-14-592

type of technical or financial assistance to local governments to support local level coastal management activities and projects.

- **Coastal habitat.** States allocated CZMP funds for coastal habitat protection and restoration activities including the acquisition or placement of easements on coastal lands; restoration of coastal habitats; data collection and mapping of coastal habitats; development of plans for habitat acquisition, restoration, and other habitat management needs; implementation of permitting and enforcement programs that protect coastal habitat through planning and regulation of development; or support of land management programs such as those for coastal preserves and parks. States also allocated CZMP funds for public outreach and education activities that focused on coastal habitat protection and restoration. According to NOAA's analysis, approximately 24 percent of CZMP funds awarded during fiscal years 2008 through 2013 were allocated to coastal habitat protection and restoration activities. According to NOAA's CZMP performance measurement system data from 2008 through 2013, states reported that they used CZMP funds to protect nearly 23,300 acres of coastal habitat through acquisition or easement, restore nearly 37,400 acres of coastal habitat, and through regulatory programs protect more than 123,000 net acres of coastal habitat.[10]

[10]CZMP performance measurement system data reported for a given year do not correspond directly with funds awarded to states in each fiscal year but can include activities completed using funding awarded for up to 3 fiscal years.

- **Coastal hazards.** States allocated CZMP funds for activities that help coastal communities minimize risks from coastal hazards, such as storms, tsunamis, and sea-level rise, and improve hazard awareness and understanding. Such activities include assessment and planning efforts, such as developing mitigation plans, risk and vulnerability assessments, and data collection and mapping to identify and manage development in areas vulnerable to coastal hazards; implementation of hazard mitigation projects; implementation and enforcement of hazard policies, regulations, and requirements; and education and training on coastal hazard topics. According to NOAA's analysis of cooperative agreements with states for CZMP funding, about 13 percent of CZMP funds awarded in fiscal years 2008 through 2013 were allocated for coastal hazards projects. The coastal hazards focus area was the one focus area where the share of CZMP funds allocated steadily increased over the 6-year period, from roughly 7 percent in fiscal year 2008 to about 16 percent in fiscal year 2013. Most state program officials we spoke with identified their work to help communities reduce future damage from hazardous events and impacts from sea-level rise related to climate change as among their more significant projects. NOAA also identified coastal hazards work as a priority area, and in 2011, through the agency's funding guidance, began encouraging states to use CZMP funding for projects that improve the resiliency of coastal communities to adapt to the impacts of coastal hazards and climate change. In addition, many of the projects that were awarded funding under the competitive Projects of Special Merit Program in fiscal years 2012 and 2013 were identified by states as addressing, at least in part, coastal hazards, according to NOAA officials.[11] For example, South Carolina's project to study tidal inlet dynamics and erosion and Maine's adaptation planning project for its coastal parks both addressed coastal hazard issues. NOAA's CZMP performance measurement system data for 2008 through 2013 show that states reported working with more than 410 communities to reduce risks from coastal hazards and nearly 230 communities to improve public awareness of coastal hazards issues.

[11]Under NOAA's Projects of Special Merit Program, states with 5-year assessment and strategy reports may submit applications for specific projects that further enhance area strategies related to select national enhancement priority areas identified by NOAA.

Estuaries—such as Sarasota Bay, that spans about 56 miles along the southwest Florida coast—are important productive ecosystems that provide habitat for a diversity of species. Nonpoint source pollution carried through runoff influences the health of the Sarasota Bay, which has limited tidal flushing, no major tr butary, and receives most of its freshwater from rainfall and associated runoff.

Florida's coastal management program provided nearly $150,000 in coastal zone funds to support a multiyear water quality monitoring and modeling study in Sarasota Bay led by the Florida Fish and Wildlife Research Institute. The study was designed to help determine major factors affecting the ecological health of the bay. Specifically, coastal zone funding was used for statistical modeling to differentiate between the effects of polluted runoff into the bay during storm events from the effects of natural algal, or other natural sources of nutrients, in the bay. Florida state program officials told us that understanding ecological responses in estuaries can facilitate planning to minimize potential impacts and help maintain overall ecosystem health. Continued water quality monitoring and modeling is being completed in the bay with other funding sources, according to Florida officials.

An aerial view of Sarasota Bay in southwest Florida shows the lagoon system with a series of barrier islands to the west.

Source: Florida Coastal Office. | GAO-14-592

- **Coastal water quality.** States allocated CZMP funds for water quality permitting and enforcement activities such as permitting of storm water discharges; activities and projects related to water quality management including vegetative plantings or other nonstructural shoreline erosion control projects; water quality monitoring; activities and projects for local governments to improve water quality management; technical assistance, data collection, mapping, planning, and policy development to address water quality issues; marine debris and other coastal cleanup or pollution prevention programs; and projects and activities that provide technical assistance to marinas to reduce nonpoint source pollution; and public outreach and education on water quality issues. Activities include those that support states in implementing their coastal nonpoint source pollution control programs. According to NOAA's CZMP performance measurement system data, from 2008 through 2013, states reported that they worked with more than 680 communities to develop nonpoint source pollution management policies and plans, or complete related projects, and removed 27 million pounds of marine debris through coastal cleanup activities.

- **Coastal community development.** States allocated CZMP funds for activities including planning and construction to support the redevelopment of urban waterfronts, ports, and harbors; technical assistance to local governments related to waterfront redevelopment; community planning, land-use planning, green infrastructure planning, and other sustainable development efforts; and public outreach and education activities specific to coastal community development issues. According to CZMP performance measurement system data from 2008 through 2013, states reported that they worked with more than 580 coastal communities to promote development and growth in ways that protect coastal resources and with more than 250 communities to redevelop ports and waterfronts.

- **Public access.** States allocated CZMP funds for activities including creating new public access sites through easements or right of ways; enhancing existing public access through trails, handicap features, or educational signage; developing plans, collecting data, and providing technical assistance to local governments on public access planning; and conducting public outreach and education activities on public access issues. According to NOAA's analysis, states allocated the least amount of CZMP funding (about 6 percent of total CZMP funding) for activities that improve public access to the coast. Unlike other focus areas, a number of states did not allocate funds for public access. According to NOAA officials, some states may not need to use CZMP funding to support public access projects, for example, because they already have sufficient public access to coastal areas. In total, according to CZMP performance measurement system data from 2008 through 2013, states reported that with CZMP funds and through regulatory programs they helped create nearly 700 new public coastal access sites and helped enhance nearly 1,500 existing sites.

State program officials told us that CZMP funding is important because it can help leverage other financial resources and provides sustained, multiyear funding for projects. We found that CZMP-funded projects and activities often involved partnerships with various entities and used multiple sources of funding. According to state program officials, CZMP funds were often the catalyst for obtaining additional financial assistance or other resources. For example, we visited a $5.2 million, multiyear marsh restoration project along the Texas Gulf coast that received nearly 20 percent of overall project funding through the CZMP and additional financial support from eight other federal, state, and private sources. Representatives from the nonprofit organization responsible for managing the project told us that CZMP funds received during the initial stages helped attract other funding partners needed for such a large-scale restoration project. Similarly, Virginia's program used $6,000 of its CZMP funding to leverage staff from six partner organizations to plan and conduct a Marine Debris Summit that laid the groundwork for developing a marine debris plan and establish priorities for future work, which state program officials expect will serve as a model for other Mid-Atlantic states. Most of the state programs we reviewed also provide competitive grants or offer other assistance to leverage local resources to address coastal issues. For example, Florida's program competitively awards a portion of its administrative funds annually through grants to coastal counties and municipalities for projects that help communities address a wide range of coastal issues, and these grants require local entities to match the state grants. Similarly, Maine's program uses CZMP funds annually to provide competitive grants to coastal communities for planning activities that support harbor management and development or improve shoreline access, but actual implementation of the projects must be funded through other sources.

## Limitations Exist with NOAA's Performance Assessment Tools, and NOAA Makes Limited Use of Performance Information

NOAA's two primary performance assessment tools, the CZMP performance measurement system and its state program evaluations, have limitations, even with changes NOAA has made since 2008, and NOAA uses the performance information it collects to a limited extent in managing the CZMP. We found that NOAA's CZMP performance measurement system does not align with some key attributes of successful performance measures. In addition, in its method for selecting stakeholders to survey during state program evaluations, NOAA may be susceptible to collecting incomplete and biased information because, in part, it uses a single criterion to select stakeholders to survey. Furthermore, NOAA makes limited use of the performance information it collects—for instance, NOAA does not use data from its performance measurement system or its evaluations of state programs to improve implementation of the CZMP at the national level—and, as a result, may not be realizing the full benefit of collecting such information.

## NOAA's CZMP Performance Measurement System Does Not Align with Some Key Attributes of Successful Performance Measures

NOAA's CZMP performance measurement system, which the agency developed in response to congressional direction to assess the national impact of the CZMP, has limitations, even with changes the agency made to the system since our 2008 report. Specifically, NOAA has made changes to several aspects of the data collection and review components of its system, including the following:

- establishing a requirement, in 2010, that state programs submit documentation of source information to support their data submissions, such as documentation of the public access sites being reported for public access performance measures;[12]
- refining, in 2009, 2010, and 2011, the names and definitions of some performance measures with the intention of clarifying the activities that a given measure is intended to capture;[13] and
- issuing internal guidance, in 2010, for NOAA staff to review state-submitted data and accompanying documentation to ensure that only eligible activities are reported by the states, among other things.[14]

With these changes, the system aligns with some key attributes of successful performance measures. In our past work, we found that successful performance measures typically align with key attributes including reliability, clarity, balance, numerical targets, and limited overlap, among others (see app. III for a complete list of key attributes we identified).[15] In our current review, we found that some of the changes

---

[12]This change was in response to our 2008 recommendation that NOAA improve its internal controls by verifying state-submitted data.

[13]For example, for a performance measure on the number of training and coordination events offered by a state program, NOAA clarified in its 2010 guidance that coordination events reported should be limited to those that are initiated or funded by a state program.

[14]This change was in response to our 2008 recommendation that NOAA improve its internal controls by verifying state-submitted data.

[15]Other key attributes of successful performance measures we have identified in our past work are: linkage, objectivity, core program activities, and government-wide priorities. See GAO, *Environmental Justice: EPA Needs to Take Additional Actions to Help Ensure Effective Implementation*, GAO-12-77 (Washington, D.C.: Oct. 6, 2011) and *Tax Administration: IRS Needs to Further Refine Its Tax Filing Season Performance Measures*, GAO-03-143 (Washington, D.C.: Nov. 22, 2002). We developed nine attributes of performance measures based on previously established GAO criteria. In addition, we considered key legislation, such as the Government Performance and Results Act of 1993 (GPRA) and the IRS Restructuring and Reform Act of 1998, and other performance management literature. Our nine attributes may not cover all the attributes of successful performance measures, but we believe these are some of the most important.

NOAA made to its CZMP performance measurement system since 2008 are consistent with such key attributes. For example, NOAA's requirement that state programs submit documentation of source information and its internal guidance for how staff are to review this documentation correspond with the key attribute of ensuring the reliability of performance measures.[16] In addition, NOAA's steps to refine the names and definitions of certain performance measures are demonstrative of the key attribute of clarity, meaning that measures are clearly stated and have names and definitions consistent with the methodology used to calculate them.

On the other hand, we found limitations in the CZMP performance measurement system that did not align with the key attributes. For instance, in 2011, NOAA eliminated its coastal water quality focus area—corresponding to one of the six focus areas based on goals of the CZMP outlined in the act. In eliminating this focus area, NOAA removed five related performance measures; states continue to report on one measure related to coastal water quality, but do so under another focus area on coastal community development. Balance, or having a set of measures that cover a program's various goals, is a key attribute of successful performance measures. We found that having measures that correspond to various program goals provided agencies with a complete picture of performance.[17] NOAA officials indicated that they eliminated the coastal water quality focus area based on a 2011 performance measurement system workgroup's recommendation to streamline the measurement system.[18] They further explained that they took this action because state programs were no longer receiving coastal nonpoint program funding, which often funded activities in support of coastal water quality, and that activities under this focus area were often tied to the coastal community development focus area. In speaking with some state program officials, however, we found that improving coastal water quality remains a priority for their programs even without coastal nonpoint program funding.

---

[16]A reliable measure is one that is calculated using standard procedures, such that the same result would likely be produced if the procedures were applied repeatedly to the same situation.

[17]GAO-12-77 and GAO-03-143.

[18]The 2011 workgroup was composed of NOAA and state program officials. It was tasked with reviewing and revising the CZMP performance measurement system to more effectively communicate program accomplishments.

GAO-14-592 Coastal Zone Management

Similarly, representatives from the Coastal States Organization's coastal water quality workgroup indicated that many state programs have made progress in developing and implementing coastal nonpoint pollution control programs, but that these results are not quantified by NOAA.

In addition, NOAA has not established numerical targets for the measures in its CZMP performance measurement system for the purpose of tracking progress or assessing performance of the CZMP. Our past work found that numerical targets are a key attribute of successful performance measures because they allow managers to compare planned performance with actual results.[19] In 2008, we recommended that NOAA establish numerical targets for performance measures that would help track progress toward meeting program goals and help assess the overall CZMP effectiveness. NOAA's 2011 performance measurement system workgroup also recommended that NOAA set targets to help it more effectively measure and communicate CZMP performance. NOAA agreed with these recommendations, but it has not established numerical targets for the measures in its CZMP performance measurement system to assess CZMP performance. NOAA officials explained that state programs vary widely, making it difficult to set targets at the national level.[20] Officials also said that they first need to review the performance measures before they assess the feasibility of developing numerical targets. NOAA officials added that NOAA has set numerical targets for four CZMP performance measures, which are included in Commerce's department-wide goals related to environmental stewardship.[21] NOAA officials told us that they considered historical performance measure data and state programs' planned strategies when establishing these targets, but they do not use them to assess CZMP performance. We continue to believe that, without

---

[19]GAO-12-77 and GAO-03-143.

[20]We have previously identified strategies to help federal programs overcome challenges in setting targets, such as developing targets based on historical performance data, trend analyses, planned strategies and program improvements, or multiyear targets, when specific annual targets cannot be identified. See: GAO, *State Small Business Credit Initiative: Opportunities Exist to Enhance Performance Measurement and Evaluation,* GAO-14-97 (Washington, D.C.: Dec. 18, 2013 and *Managing for Results: Strengthening Regulatory Agencies' Performance Management Practices,* GAO/GGD-00-10 (Washington, D.C.: Oct. 28, 1999).

[21]Data from four CZMP performance measures—one coastal habitat measure, two coastal hazards measures, and one coastal community development measure—along with data from other NOAA programs are used to support two department-wide performance measures established under the GPRA Modernization Act.

setting numerical targets for the CZMP performance measurement system, NOAA will not have a benchmark to help it determine the extent to which the CZMP may be meeting expectations.

Finally, the CZMP performance measurement system includes performance measures that involve the collection of data by state programs that are already available to NOAA from other sources. Limited overlap, another key attribute of successful performance measures, notes that measures should produce new information beyond what is provided by other data sources and that redundant or unnecessary performance information costs resources and clouds the bottom line by making managers sort through excess information.[22] We found that the CZMP performance measurement system includes at least two financial measures whereby states collect and submit financial expenditure data similar to data states already provide NOAA through their cooperative agreements.[23] NOAA officials told us that, in developing the CZMP performance measurement system, they anticipated that including such measures would be useful for tracking the amount of CZMP funding used in different focus areas each year. However, NOAA used the financial information from its CZMP performance measurement system to prepare a one-time summary of performance measure data published in 2013. In contrast, it uses financial information drawn from cooperative agreements on an annual basis to analyze states' planned uses of CZMP funding. NOAA officials acknowledged that they may need to review the utility of requiring state programs to collect financial expenditure data for the performance measurement system. By requiring states to collect and submit financial data similar to data that they already provide in their cooperative agreements and making limited use of these data, NOAA

---

[22]GAO-12-77 and GAO-03-143.

[23]The two measures require states to submit 20 individual pieces of financial data into the CZMP performance measurement system. One measure requires state programs to report the amount of CZMP funds and state matching funds spent in five different focus areas, such as public access and coastal habitat. A second measure requires states to report on CZMP funds and state matching funds provided to local governments in the form of financial and technical assistance by focus area. Because state programs have 3 years after funds are awarded to obligate CZMP funds before they must be returned to NOAA, data reported annually by states in the CZMP performance measurement system may include funds awarded from up to 3 prior fiscal years. Financial information from states' cooperative agreements, on the other hand, corresponds to states' planned uses of funds in the upcoming fiscal year.

may be unnecessarily burdening state programs with data collection requirements.

Several state program officials we interviewed told us that collecting data for the numerous data elements under the 17 performance measures is a time- and resource-intensive activity, with a few stating that this is particularly true relative to the amount of CZMP funds they receive. Some indicated, for instance, that they spend 30 staff days or more per year collecting these data. State officials said that, in particular, data for the financial measures are among the most time-consuming to collect and report to NOAA. Other state officials told us that collecting data on the number of educational and training events and participants for each focus area is especially time-consuming, with one official noting that collecting data on number of participants is particularly burdensome when events are hosted by parties other than the program itself.

NOAA officials told us they recognized the need to continue to review and potentially streamline or revise the CZMP performance measurement system, and that they intend to do so once the merger of OCRM and the Coastal Services Center is complete, which they expect to occur by the end of 2014. In the interim, NOAA officials said they initiated at the beginning of fiscal year 2014 an effort to assess all performance measures collected by the various programs within the two offices, including the CZMP, to determine which measures may be most effective in tracking and communicating progress toward goals identified in the merged office's strategic plan. NOAA officials said they are committed to developing a strong framework for evaluating the performance of all programs under its merged coastal management office. However, the agency has not documented the approach it plans to take for these efforts. Federal internal control standards state the need for federal agencies to establish plans that encompass actions the agency will take to help ensure goals and objectives can be met.[24] Without a documented approach for how it plans to assess its CZMP performance measurement system—including the scope and criteria it will use, such as how it will ensure its measures align with key attributes of successful performance measures—NOAA cannot demonstrate that its intended effort will improve its CZMP performance measurement system.

---

[24]GAO, *Standards for Internal Control in the Federal Government*, GAO/AIMD-00-21.3.1 (Washington, D.C.: November 1999).

## NOAA Cannot Ensure That Its Revised Process for Surveying Stakeholders to Inform State Program Evaluations Will Produce Complete and Unbiased Information

In 2013, NOAA revised its process for conducting state program evaluations, which are required under the Coastal Zone Management Act to assess state programs' adherence to the act's requirements, but we identified a limitation in NOAA's method for sampling stakeholders under the revised process. According to NOAA documents, the purpose of the revisions was to conduct evaluations more efficiently, at a reduced cost, while continuing to meet evaluation requirements outlined in the act.[25] In revising its state program evaluations, NOAA made changes in the timing and methods for collecting information from participating states (see table 4). A NOAA official estimates that the agency's revised evaluation process will save the agency approximately $236,000 annually. NOAA began evaluating state programs using its revised process at the beginning of fiscal year 2014 with evaluations of seven state programs. We did not evaluate NOAA's implementation of its revised state program evaluations because NOAA had not completed its first cycle at the time of our review and, therefore, it was too early to assess the effectiveness of its revisions. However, we did assess NOAA's revised evaluation design against our and others' work on program evaluations to identify standards for strong evaluation design.[26] We were unable to evaluate the qualitative components of its revised evaluation design—including the change in the scope of the evaluations from NOAA's review of all aspects of each state program to a review of a few areas determined by NOAA—because the results of using these methods cannot be fully assessed until the evaluations have been conducted. But, we did evaluate the steps NOAA laid out in its guidance on its methods for collecting information and identified a limitation in its method for sampling stakeholders to survey.

---

[25]Under the act, state program evaluations are to examine the extent to which states have: (1) implemented their approved programs; (2) addressed coastal management needs identified in the act; and (3) adhered to the terms of CZMP funds awarded through cooperative agreements. 16 U.S.C. § 1458(a).

[26]GAO, *Designing Evaluations: 2012 Revision*, GAO-12-208G (Washington, D.C.: January 2012) and Office of Management and Budget, *Standards and Guidelines for Statistical Surveys* (Washington, D.C.: September 2006).

**Table 4: Components of the National Oceanic and Atmospheric Administration's (NOAA) Former and Revised Evaluations of State Coastal Management Programs**

| Evaluation component | Former evaluation process | Revised evaluation process |
|---|---|---|
| Frequency of evaluations | Each state program evaluated every 3 years; 11 evaluations conducted per year | Each state program evaluated every 5 years; 7 evaluations conducted per year |
| Scope | Evaluations consider all aspects of program requirements in equal depth | Evaluations focus on three "target areas," which are recurring or major issues facing a state program or innovative or high impact projects being undertaken; other program requirements are also considered |
| Timing of information collection | NOAA collects information from state programs immediately before and during the site visit | NOAA collects documents and answers from state programs on a standard set of questions early in the evaluation process to help determine evaluation target areas and inform other aspects of the evaluation |
| Methods for information collection | In-person site visits and interviews conducted for each evaluation<br><br>Stakeholders provide information during site visit meetings | In-person site visits conducted for up to two evaluations per year<br><br>Stakeholders provide information through surveys and interviews, either by telephone/video-conference for evaluations without site visits, or in-person for evaluations with site visits |
| Use of quantitative data | No state-specific quantitative performance measures included in evaluations | NOAA reviews progress toward three state-specific performance measures and numerical targets as part of evaluations[a] |
| Findings document | 30 to over 50 pages in length | 5 to 10 pages in length |

Source: GAO analysis of NOAA information. | GAO-14-592

[a]NOAA required each state program to develop three state-specific performance measures and targets to address a recommendation from our 2008 report that NOAA establish performance goals to evaluate state programs. Evaluation target areas and targets associated with state-specific performance measures have no relationship to one another. NOAA's guidance says that it is coincidental that it chose to use the term "target area" within the evaluation context and the term "target" as one component of an evaluation performance measure.

Under its revised evaluation process, NOAA relies in part on information obtained through stakeholder surveys, but we found that through its method of sampling stakeholders to survey, the agency may be susceptible to collecting incomplete and biased information. According to NOAA guidance on its revised evaluations, stakeholder surveys are intended to provide information about stakeholders' perspectives and opinions across a range of topics, from a state program's top three strengths and weaknesses to opportunities for improving a program's federal consistency and permitting processes. The guidance states that NOAA will use stakeholder survey responses to identify evaluation target areas, as well as obtain information about the extent to which a state program is performing effectively in areas outside of the target areas. NOAA officials indicated that they plan to analyze survey results by collating respondents' answers to identify common themes. NOAA evaluators will identify a sample of stakeholders to survey from 12 categories of organizations that stakeholders represent, including federal agencies, state agencies, nonprofit organizations, academic institutions, and local businesses and industries. According to NOAA officials, they adopted the criterion of stakeholder categories to ensure that stakeholders whose views were not consistently represented in the former evaluations—such as those from local businesses and industries—are included in evaluations conducted under the revised process. NOAA evaluators will select stakeholders to survey from these 12 categories from a list of potential stakeholders to survey compiled by state program officials and NOAA specialists working with the state.

According to the Office of Management and Budget's Standards and Guidelines for Statistical Surveys, a survey sampling method should yield the data required to meet the objectives of the survey.[27] Our previous work has found that strong program evaluations rely on data that sufficiently reflect the activities and conditions a program is expected to address.[28] Because NOAA's stakeholder sampling method is guided by one criterion—categories of stakeholder organizations—NOAA may not collect information that reflects the various activities and aspects of the state programs. Specifically, under the act, NOAA is required to evaluate the extent to which state programs have addressed coastal management needs reflecting the six focus areas based on the goals identified in the act. In the absence of additional criteria for selecting stakeholders to survey, NOAA may select a sample of stakeholders whose work with a state program does not span all of the act's goals, potentially leaving NOAA without information to inform its evaluation of a state's performance on one or more goals. Such an information gap could be significant because stakeholder surveys are intended to be a main source of information on how well a program is performing in areas beyond those identified as target areas.

---

[27] Office of Management and Budget, *Standards and Guidelines for Statistical Surveys* (Washington, D.C.: September 2006).

[28] GAO-12-208G.

Furthermore, when using a nonprobabilistic sampling method, such as that being employed by NOAA for its stakeholder surveys, the Office of Management and Budget's survey guidelines state that agencies should demonstrate that they used an impartial, objective method to include or exclude people or organizations from a sample. Our previous work on program evaluation also found that evaluation data should be sufficiently free of bias or other errors that could lead to inaccurate conclusions.[29] Because state program officials responsible for identifying potential stakeholders to survey have a vested interest in their programs, NOAA's process is susceptible to collecting biased information. NOAA specialists who work with state programs also contribute to the selection process. However, we found that some NOAA specialists are not regionally located or have worked with a state program for a short period of time and, therefore, their knowledge or experience to inform the selection process may be limited. NOAA's evaluation guidance recognizes the need to assess its revised process in the future and states that the agency plans to evaluate the effectiveness and efficiency of its revised state program evaluation process after conducting 8 to 10 evaluations.

## NOAA Makes Limited Use of Performance Data It Collects in Managing the CZMP

We found that in managing the CZMP, NOAA makes limited use of the performance information it collects. Our past work has found that performance information can be used across a range of management functions to improve programs and results, including to (1) identify problems or weaknesses in programs and take corrective actions, (2) set program priorities and develop strategies, (3) recognize and reward organizations who meet or exceed expectations, and (4) identify and share effective approaches to program implementation.[30] For example, our previous work found that the Department of Labor effectively used performance measure data to identify technical assistance needs of state programs and to then provide assistance to try to improve performance. The department also used performance measure data as a basis for providing financial incentives to state programs that receive federal grants. We found that agencies realize the full benefit of collecting

---

[29]GAO-12-208G.

[30]GAO, *Managing for Results: Enhancing Agency Use of Performance Information for Management Decision Making*, GAO-05-927 (Washington, D.C.: Sept. 9, 2005) and *Managing for Results: Executive Branch Should More Fully Implement the GPRA Modernization Act to Address Pressing Governance Challenges*, GAO-13-518 (Washington, D.C.: June 26, 2013).

GAO-14-592 Coastal Zone Management

performance information only when they use such information to make decisions designed to improve results.

NOAA collects performance information through its CZMP performance measurement system, state program evaluations, and other sources, but we found that the agency generally does not use the information it collects to help manage the CZMP at a national level. Specifically, we found the following:

- *NOAA uses its CZMP performance measurement system data to report on national program accomplishments on a limited basis.* In particular, in 2013, NOAA produced one report summarizing performance measurement system data from 2008 through 2011.[31] However, NOAA has not published additional similar reports, and has not used performance measurement system data for other purposes. For example, the agency has not used the performance measurement system data to identify potential problems or weaknesses in the CZMP, set program priorities or strategies, or recognize and reward high-performing state programs—which may limit the usefulness of collecting such data.

- *NOAA does not use its state program evaluations to assess the performance or improve the implementation of the CZMP at the national level.* NOAA uses its state program evaluations to identify state-specific accomplishments and encourage or require the state under evaluation to make improvements or take corrective actions. But, according to NOAA officials, the agency does not regularly analyze findings from individual state evaluations to identify and share effective approaches across states or to identify common performance weaknesses that may warrant national focus or assistance.[32] Our analysis of recent NOAA evaluations of the seven state programs we reviewed found that NOAA recommended the states undertake similar actions. In five of the seven state program

---

[31]The report provides examples of results achieved by the CZMP, such as creation of 470 new public access sites in support of the CZMP goal to create and enhance public access to coastal areas, and protection of 14,500 acres of coastal habitat between 2008 and 2011, in support of the CZMP goal to protect coastal habitat through acquisition or easement.

[32]In 2007, NOAA produced a summary of findings from state program evaluation reports that were issued in fiscal year 2006. NOAA officials said they no longer have the capacity to prepare such a summary due to limited staffing and other resource constraints.

evaluations, for example, NOAA recommended that programs undertake strategic planning, and for four of the seven programs, NOAA recommended that programs improve their coordination with local governments or other partners who help carry out coastal management activities. Yet NOAA has not analyzed these evaluations to identify common findings. One NOAA specialist we spoke with suggested that NOAA could also use the results of its state program evaluations to recognize and reward high-performing state programs. For instance, the NOAA specialist suggested that NOAA could modify its eligibility requirements for its Projects of Special Merit funding such that only high-performing programs, with any necessary actions from past state program evaluations fully implemented, would be eligible to receive funding.

- *NOAA does not use performance-related information from other sources to support its management of the CZMP.* NOAA uses state programs' semiannual progress reports—which contain, among other things, "success stories," or examples of a state program successfully addressing coastal management issues[33]—to track states' progress in implementing their cooperative agreements. However, NOAA does not use information from these reports to identify and promote effective approaches to coastal management by regularly sharing states' success stories across states or with other stakeholders. The 2011 performance measurement system workgroup composed of NOAA and state program officials recommended that NOAA develop a website to share success stories on an annual basis. NOAA did not implement this recommendation because, according to NOAA officials, at that time it was incorporating success stories into a quarterly newsletter. According to a NOAA document, the agency produced the newsletter in response to requests from states for more information about how other state programs address coastal management issues. NOAA stopped issuing this newsletter in 2012, when its office merger began, and NOAA officials said they are now evaluating how the merged office might best share information about the CZMP across state programs and with other stakeholders.

NOAA's strategic plan for its merged coastal management office recognizes the importance of using and reporting performance

---

[33]For example, according to an example from NOAA, a success story from Virginia's program describes how the program's coordination and research efforts helped facilitate the passage of state legislation protecting dunes and beaches.

information. According to this plan, NOAA is committed to maintaining a culture of monitoring and evaluation to improve the implementation of its programs. We found, however, that the strategic plan does not include a documented strategy for using the performance data NOAA collects through its CZMP performance measurement system, state program evaluations, or other sources of information, such as states' semiannual progress reports, to manage the CZMP. NOAA officials told us that because the office merger is under way, they have not formulated a strategy for how the merged office will use performance data to inform and manage the CZMP, but they recognized the need to do so once the merger is complete. Federal control standards state the need for federal agencies to document management approaches to ensure goals and objectives can be met.[34] Without a documented strategy for using the full range of performance information it collects, NOAA may not be taking full advantage of the performance information that its specialists, evaluators, and state program officials spend time and resources collecting, and it cannot ensure that it is realizing the full benefit of collecting such information, such as identifying common problems in state programs and taking corrective actions, setting national program priorities and developing strategies, recognizing state programs that exceed expectations, or identifying and sharing effective approaches to program implementation.

Finally, NOAA has not taken steps to integrate data from its CZMP performance measurement system with information from its state program evaluations to develop a complete picture of the CZMP's performance, as we recommended in our 2008 report. In 2008, we found that NOAA was not integrating quantitative national performance measure data with qualitative information from state program evaluations to develop a more comprehensive assessment of the CZMP's performance. NOAA agreed with our recommendation to develop an approach for integrating the two types of information and, in response, tasked the 2011 performance measurement system workgroup with developing a method for better communicating performance measure data. The workgroup recommended a template for communicating program results that includes quantitative national performance measure data and qualitative success stories from states' semiannual progress reports. However, NOAA has not drawn on this quantitative and qualitative information for

---

[34]GAO/AIMD-00-21.3.1.

purposes other than producing a report in 2013 summarizing performance measurement system data. Specifically, NOAA has not integrated quantitative and qualitative information to better understand program performance, improve its assessment of difficult-to-measure activities, or validate its assessments of program progress. We have previously found that agencies that used multiple sources of data to assess performance had information that covered more aspects of program performance than those that relied on a single source.[35] We also found that agencies can improve their performance assessments by using program evaluation information to validate performance measurement system data.[36] We continue to believe that developing an approach to combine performance information from its CZMP performance measurement system and state program evaluations could help NOAA obtain a more complete picture of CZMP performance.

## Conclusions

The CZMP plays an integral role in helping states protect, restore, and manage the development of the nation's coastal resources and habitats. In managing the CZMP, NOAA is challenged with the task of assessing the performance of the program, composed of partnerships with 34 individual states, each with unique coastal habitats, and differing laws, organizational structures, and funding priorities. NOAA is to be commended for its progress in improving its two primary performance assessment tools—its CZMP performance measurement system and state program evaluations—since we last reviewed the agency's performance assessment processes in 2008. We are encouraged by NOAA's recognition of the importance of using performance information to improve the implementation of the CZMP. However, NOAA does not use or have a documented strategy for how it will use the performance information it collects from its CZMP performance measurement system, state program evaluations, or other sources of performance-related information, as appropriate, to aid its management of the CZMP. Without a documented strategy for using the range of its performance information, NOAA cannot ensure that it is collecting the most meaningful information and realizing the full benefit of the significant amount of information it and

[35]GAO, *Managing for Results: Challenges Agencies Face in Producing Credible Performance Information*, GAO/GGD-00-52 (Washington, D.C.: Feb. 4, 2000).

[36]GAO, *Program Evaluation: Studies Helped Agencies Measure or Explain Program Performance*, GAO/GGD-00-204 (Washington, D.C.: Sept. 29, 2000).

the states collect, such as identifying common problems in state programs and taking corrective actions, setting national program priorities and developing strategies, recognizing state programs that exceed expectations, or identifying and sharing effective approaches to program implementation.

We also are encouraged by NOAA's intentions to review and possibly revise the CZMP performance measurement system once its new coastal office is in place, but the agency has yet to document the approach it plans to take—including the scope and criteria it will use for this effort. In the absence of a documented approach indicating how it will review its performance measurement system, NOAA cannot ensure that its upcoming effort will take into consideration key attributes of successful performance measures, including balance and limited overlap, or result in a system that provides meaningful information that can be used by NOAA to determine how effectively the CZMP is performing relative to its goals. We are further encouraged by NOAA's commitment to evaluate the effectiveness and efficiency of its revised state program evaluation process and to modify it, as needed, as it moves forward with its implementation. In the interim, however, NOAA's method for selecting stakeholders to survey during state program evaluations—which relies on a single criterion and on state program officials who have a vested interest in the program—may result in the collection of incomplete or biased information that does not ensure perspectives are gathered from stakeholders representing a variety of program goals and are collected in an objective manner, potentially undermining the sufficiency and credibility of the data the produces. In the absence of additional criteria for selecting stakeholders to survey, NOAA may select a sample of stakeholders whose work with a state program does not span the act's six focus areas or who present less-than-objective assessments of a state program.

## Recommendations for Executive Action

To ensure that NOAA collects and uses meaningful performance information to help manage the CZMP, including continuing to improve its CZMP performance measurement system and its state program evaluations, we are recommending that the Secretary of Commerce direct the Administrator of NOAA to take the following three actions:

- Develop a documented strategy to use the range of performance information the agency collects, as appropriate, to aid its management of the CZMP, such as to identify potential problems or weaknesses in the CZMP; set program priorities or strategies; or recognize and reward high-performing state programs.

- As part of its intended review of the CZMP performance measurement system and in consideration of how it intends to use the performance information, document the approach it plans to take to analyze and revise, as appropriate, the performance measures, and in so doing ensure the analysis considers key attributes of successful performance measures, such as balance and limited overlap.

- Revise the sampling methodology for selecting stakeholders to survey—included as part of its state program evaluation process—to ensure perspectives are gathered from stakeholders representing a variety of program goals and are collected in an objective manner.

## Agency Comments and Our Evaluation

We provided a draft of this report to the Department of Commerce for review and comment. In written comments provided by NOAA through Commerce (reproduced in appendix IV), NOAA generally agreed with our findings and concurred with our recommendations. NOAA also provided technical comments that we incorporated, as appropriate. In its comment letter, NOAA stated that while it found GAO's evaluation of the CZMP performance measurement system accurate, the agency did not agree with GAO's assessment that eliminating a stand-alone category for coastal water quality could negatively affect the system's ability to reflect the goals of the CZMA in a balanced way. NOAA stated that removal of the coastal water quality focus area did not impair its ability to track progress in meeting the water quality goal of the CZMA, explaining that it retained one measure composed of two data elements related to coastal water quality, but housed under a different focus area. We agree that the two-part measure NOAA maintained related to coastal water quality may provide important information on performance in this area. However, we continue to believe that the information it is collecting related to coastal water quality may not be balanced in comparison to the information it is collecting for the other five focus areas, which could in turn result in inconsistent performance information when looking across the six focus areas of the program. NOAA concurred with the three recommendations in the report and described actions it plans to address them. With regard to the first recommendation, NOAA stated that it plans to develop a strategy for using performance information it collects, including information from its performance measurement system, evaluations of state programs, performance reports, and other sources, and noted that it will build upon existing efforts to share lessons-learned regarding successful approaches or shared challenges across the national program. In addressing our second recommendation, on documenting its approach for analyzing and revising, as appropriate, the performance measures, NOAA stated that it plans to conduct a review of CZMP performance measures in fiscal year 2015 as part of its ongoing analysis of performance measures for programs under its new coastal office. In response to our third recommendation, NOAA stated that it will revise its sampling methodology to ensure stakeholders representing a variety of program goals are selected.

We are sending copies of this report to the Secretary of Commerce, the appropriate congressional committees, and other interested parties. In addition, the report is available at no charge on the GAO website at http://www.gao.gov.

If you or your staff members have any questions about this report, please contact me at (202) 512-3841 or fennella@gao.gov. Contact points for our Offices of Congressional Relations and Public Affairs may be found on the last page of this report. GAO staff who made major contributions to this report are listed in appendix V.

Anne-Marie Fennell
Director, Natural Resources and Environment

# Appendix I:  Objectives, Scope, and Methodology

Focusing on National Coastal Zone Management Program (CZMP) activities since our 2008 report, our objectives were to examine (1) how participating states allocated CZMP funds awarded in fiscal years 2008 through 2013 and (2) how the National Oceanic and Atmospheric Administration's (NOAA) primary performance assessment tools have changed and the extent to which NOAA uses performance information to help manage the CZMP.

To examine how participating states allocated CZMP funds awarded in fiscal years 2008 through 2013, we reviewed the Coastal Zone Management Act and related regulations and guidance, including NOAA funding guidance and allocation memos. We analyzed NOAA data on federal funds awarded by state and by funding type from fiscal years 2008 to 2013, and we compared this data against annual NOAA funding guidance and allocation memorandums to states. Based on our analysis, and interviews with NOAA officials, we found the data to be sufficiently reliable. We reviewed NOAA's analysis of states' allocations of CZMP funding for fiscal years 2008 through 2013, which was based on NOAA's review of its cooperative agreements for federal funding with states. NOAA's analysis involved the categorization of states' funding allocations for projects into six focus areas based on the goals of the act and an additional state program management category as defined by NOAA to cover administrative costs, such as general program operations, supplies, and rent. NOAA officials noted that total funding allocation amounts are approximate and that many CZMP funded activities could address more than one focus area. For example, Maine state program officials told us their activities to conserve and enhance properties that provide commercial fishing access address both coastal community development and public access focus areas. To address this challenge, NOAA developed written guidance for NOAA specialists who conduct the analysis that specifies the types of activities to include in each focus area and the state program management category, as well as direction on how to categorize funds in cases where a project or activity may fall in more than one category. For instance, NOAA defined funds in the government coordination focus area to include, among others, activities that involved coordination with other government agencies and stakeholders, technical assistance to local governments, or public outreach and education activities only if they did not correspond to other focus areas. To determine the reliability of NOAA's analysis, we interviewed knowledgeable NOAA officials, reviewed NOAA's process for categorizing proposed activities and projects, including its written guidance on categorizing CZMP-funded activities and its steps to compare funding amounts to ensure that the double-counting of funds did not take place.

We did not independently verify the results of NOAA's analysis, but we verified major categories used in NOAA's analysis for consistency across years, checked the total allocated funds in NOAA's analysis against total federal funding award data, and reviewed NOAA's categorization of a small sample of projects. We concluded the data to be sufficiently reliable for our purposes of reporting states' allocated uses of CZMP funds.

We also reviewed data from NOAA's CZMP performance measurement system from 2008 through 2013 (the most recent years for which data was available) to further illustrate how CZMP funds were used. To assess the reliability of NOAA's CZMP performance measurement system data, we interviewed NOAA officials about reliability of the data and reviewed corresponding documentation including performance measures guidance to states and internal guidance to NOAA specialists about their required reviews of data submitted. We did not independently verify performance measure data submitted by state programs, but based on our review of steps taken by NOAA to review state-submitted data, we found the data sufficiently reliable for the purposes of our report.

To examine how NOAA's primary performance assessment tools have changed since 2008, and the extent to which NOAA uses performance information to help manage the CZMP, we analyzed applicable laws and guidance including the act, and NOAA's guidance on its CZMP performance measurement system and state program evaluations. We reviewed documentation on changes NOAA has made to these two performance tools, including steps taken to address our 2008 report recommendations,[1] and we interviewed NOAA officials about the changes they made and their use of performance information. We reviewed GAO's work on performance measurement to identify key attributes associated with successful performance measures[2] and assessed NOAA's CZMP performance measurement system against these attributes by reviewing the agency's performance measures and guidance on the system and interviewing NOAA and state program officials. We also analyzed NOAA's CZMP performance measurement system data from 2011, 2012, and 2013. We reviewed our and others' work on program evaluations to

---

[1]GAO-08-1045.

[2]GAO-12-77 and GAO-03-143.

identify standards for strong evaluation design[3] and assessed NOAA's
process for evaluating state coastal programs against these standards by
examining NOAA's evaluation guidance and interviewing NOAA officials.
We examined information NOAA maintains on CZMP performance
including fact sheets, states' cooperative agreements, semiannual
progress reports, performance measurement system data submitted by
states, and state program evaluation reports.

In conducting our work on both objectives, we interviewed representatives
of the Coastal States Organization, a nonprofit organization that
represents coastal states on legislative and policy issues, as well as state
program officials from the seven states that received the most fiscal year
2012 CZMP funding in each of NOAA's seven regions (California, Florida,
Hawaii, Maine, Michigan, Texas, and Virginia) about how states used
CZMP funds and for their perspectives on NOAA's management and
assessment of the overall national program. We also reviewed the seven
states' cooperative agreements and semiannual progress reports for
fiscal years 2011 and 2012 (the most recent years for which reports were
available) to learn about projects undertaken by these seven states. We
selected one CZMP-funded project in each of the seven states to further
determine and illustrate how states used funds on a project-level basis
and to learn about how the results of a select project are captured by
NOAA's performance assessment tools. In selecting projects to review,
we considered the amount of CZMP funds allocated to specific projects,
funding type, project type (e.g., projects that provide financial and
technical assistance to local governments, planning projects,
construction-related projects, permitting activities), and focus area (e.g.,
coastal habitat, government coordination). Our review of the states'
information cannot be generalized across all states or projects. We also
interviewed coastal program officials from American Samoa and the
Northern Mariana Islands to obtain perspectives from territories on
NOAA's performance assessment tools and territories' use of this
performance information.

We conducted two site visits to observe and learn more about CZMP
projects—one to a coastal habitat restoration project in Texas and one to
an ocean planning project in Virginia. We selected these projects for site

---

[3]GAO-12-208G and Office of Management and Budget, *Standards and Guidelines for
Statistical Surveys* (Washington, D.C.: September 2006).

visits considering project type, focus area addressed, and geographic location. During our site visits, we met with state program officials and also interviewed stakeholders involved in the selected projects, as well as stakeholders involved in other CZMP-funded projects. In Texas, we met with the nonprofit organization managing the coastal habitat restoration project and toured the restoration site; in Virginia, we visited a public access enhancement project that received CZMP funding.

We conducted this performance audit from June 2013 to July 2014 in accordance with generally accepted government auditing standards. Those standards require that we plan and perform the audit to obtain sufficient, appropriate evidence to provide a reasonable basis for our findings and conclusions based on our audit objectives. We believe that the evidence obtained provides a reasonable basis for our findings and conclusions based on our audit objectives.

# Appendix II: National Coastal Zone Management Program (CZMP) Performance Measurement System Summary Data

The National Oceanic and Atmospheric Administration's (NOAA) CZMP performance measurement system is organized by broad focus areas that are related to five of the six primary focus areas based on the goals of the CZMP as outlined in the Coastal Zone Management Act. The system consists of 17 performance measures—15 of the 17 measures are organized under the five broad focus areas (NOAA removed the sixth focus area, coastal water quality, from its performance measurement system in 2011 in response to a performance measurement system workgroup's recommendation to streamline the system), and the remaining 2 measures are to track state financial expenditures. Each of the 17 measures is composed of several individual data elements. For example, the performance measure on federal consistency is composed of two data elements that track the number of projects reviewed and the number of projects modified under states' federal consistency review processes. In addition, some data elements are further broken down into specific categories, such as types of federal consistency projects modified. See table 5 for a list of the performance measures and supporting data elements and categories, as reported by participating state programs for 2011 through 2013.

Table 5: Summary of National Coastal Zone Management Program (CZMP) Performance Measurement System Data, 2011 through 2013[a]

| | 2011 | 2012 | 2013 |
|---|---|---|---|
| **Focus area: Government Coordination** | | | |
| **Performance measure 1: Federal Consistency** | | | |
| Total number of federal consistency projects technically reviewed (determined to be applicable for federal consistency review) during the reporting period | 6,767 | 7,014 | 6,540 |
| Number of federal consistency projects modified due to consultation with the applicant to meet coastal zone management policies, by category: | | | |
| Number of federal agency activity projects | 99 | 138 | 105 |
| Number of federal license or permit activity projects | 629 | 529 | 504 |
| Number of outer continental shelf projects | 0 | 0 | 0 |
| Number of projects for federal financial assistance to state agencies or local governments | 19 | 27 | 99 |
| Total number: | 747 | 694 | 708 |
| **Performance measure 2: CZMP Regulatory Habitat Protection** | | | |
| Number of acres of habitat estimated to have been lost by permit due to activities subject to coastal zone management regulatory programs, by category: | | | |

| | 2011 | 2012 | 2013 |
|---|---|---|---|
| Number of acres of tidal (or Great Lakes) wetlands | 1,384 | 417 | 499 |
| Number of acres of beach and dune habitat | 18 | 43 | 50 |
| Number of acres of nearshore habitat (intertidal, subtidal, submerged) | 298 | 2,858 | 8,864 |
| Number of acres of other habitat types | 3,413 | 2,106 | 3,690 |
| Total number: | 5,112 | 5,423 | 13,102 |

| Number of acres of habitat estimated to have been gained or mitigated due to activities subject to coastal zone management regulatory programs, by category: | | | |
|---|---|---|---|
| Number of acres of tidal (or Great Lake) wetlands | 437 | 917 | 916 |
| Number of acres of beach and dune habitat | 10 | 567 | 671 |
| Number of acres of nearshore habitat (intertidal, subtidal, submerged) | 220 | 892 | 160 |
| Number of acres of other habitat types | 76,630 | 20,359 | 30,070 |
| Total number: | 77,298 | 22,736 | 31,817 |

| Performance measure 3: Coordination Events | | | |
|---|---|---|---|
| Number of coordination events offered by state programs, by category: | | | |
| Number of government coordination events | 587 | 475 | 1,236 |
| Number of public access coordination events | 51 | 108 | 88 |
| Number of coastal habitat coordination events | 233 | 155 | 247 |
| Number of coastal hazards coordination events | 83 | 99 | 187 |
| Number of coastal community development coordination events | 138 | 126 | 161 |
| Total number: | 1,092 | 963 | 1,919 |

| Number of stakeholder groups participating in coordination events offered by state programs, by category: | | | |
|---|---|---|---|
| Number of stakeholder groups participating in government coordination events | 2,808 | 5,578 | 6,861 |
| Number of stakeholder groups participating in public access coordination events | 386 | 507 | 439 |
| Number of stakeholder groups participating in coastal habitat coordination events | 1,410 | 962 | 1,748 |
| Number of stakeholder groups participating in coastal hazards coordination events | 773 | 1,268 | 1,516 |
| Number of stakeholder groups participating in coastal community development coordination events | 1,312 | 2,203 | 1,627 |
| Total number: | 6,689 | 10,518 | 12,191 |

| Performance measure 4: Education and Training | | | |
|---|---|---|---|
| Number of educational activities related to government coordination offered by state programs | 450 | 148 | 141 |
| Number of participants in educational activities related to government coordination offered by state programs | 25,482 | 10,105 | 15,531 |

| | 2011 | 2012 | 2013 |
|---|---|---|---|
| Number of training events related to government coordination offered by state programs | 118 | 85 | 51 |
| Number of participants in training events related to government coordination offered by state programs | 2,945 | 1,980 | 1,113 |

### Focus area: Public Access

#### Performance measure 5: 306A Programs

| | 2011 | 2012 | 2013 |
|---|---|---|---|
| Number of public access sites created through acquisition or easement with assistance from CZMP funding or state program staff | 15 | 22 | 9 |
| Number of existing public access sites enhanced with assistance from CZMP funding or state program staff | 106 | 207 | 122 |

#### Performance measure 6: Public Access Regulatory Programs

| | 2011 | 2012 | 2013 |
|---|---|---|---|
| Number of public access sites created through coastal zone management regulatory requirements | 128 | 105 | 92 |
| Number of public access sites enhanced through coastal zone management regulatory requirements | 252 | 218 | 212 |

#### Performance measure 7: Public Access Education and Training

| | 2011 | 2012 | 2013 |
|---|---|---|---|
| Number of educational activities related to public access offered by state programs | 73 | 51 | 71 |
| Number of participants in educational activities related to public access offered by state programs | 16,590 | 4,655 | 10,360 |
| Number of training events related to public access offered by state programs | 4 | 36 | 20 |
| Number of participants in training events related to public access offered by state programs | 43 | 443 | 294 |

### Focus area: Coastal Habitat

#### Performance measure 8: Habitat Protected and Restored

| | 2011 | 2012 | 2013 |
|---|---|---|---|
| Number of acres of coastal habitats protected by acquisition or easement with assistance from CZMP funding or state program staff, by category: | | | |
| Number of acres of tidal or Great Lakes wetlands | 1,054 | 247 | 216 |
| Number of acres of beach and dune habitat | 0 | 0 | 0 |

GAO-14-592 Coastal Zone Management

| | 2011 | 2012 | 2013 |
|---|---|---|---|
| Number of acres of nearshore habitat (intertidal, subtidal, submerged) | 319 | 16 | 217 |
| Number of acres of other types of habitat | 1,496 | 2,841 | 5,241 |
| Total number: | 2,870 | 3,104 | 5,673 |
| **Number of meters of coastal habitats protected by acquisition or easement with assistance from CZMP funding or state program staff, by category:** | | | |
| Number of meters of beach and dune habitat | 48 | 0 | 0 |
| Number of meters of nearshore habitat (intertidal, subtidal, submerged) | 0 | 0 | 461,341 |
| Number of meters of other types of habitat | 335 | 2,589,988 | 1,623,188 |
| Total number: | 383 | 2,589,988 | 2,084,529 |
| **Number of acres of coastal habitats under restoration with assistance from CZMP funding or state program staff, by category:** | | | |
| Number of acres of tidal or Great Lakes wetlands | 3,169 | 1,544 | 5,135 |
| Number of acres of beach and dune habitat | 1,100 | 1,456 | 261 |
| Number of acres of nearshore habitat (intertidal, subtidal, submerged) | 407 | 68 | 162 |
| Number of acres of other types of habitat | 1,342 | 292 | 469 |
| Total number: | 6,018 | 3,359 | 6,027 |
| **Number of meters of coastal habitats under restoration with assistance from CZMP funding or state program staff, by category:** | | | |
| Number of meters of beach and dune habitat | 21,929 | 220 | 5,829 |
| Number of meters of nearshore habitat (intertidal, subtidal, submerged) | 0 | 2,089 | 1,411 |
| Number of meters of other types of habitat | 47,167 | 2,333 | 28,534 |
| Total number: | 69,096 | 4,642 | 35,774 |
| **Performance measure 9: Marine Debris Removal** | | | |
| Number of marine debris removal activities completed with assistance from CZMP funding or state program staff | 3,667 | 2,444 | 2,879 |
| Estimated number of pounds of debris removed by the above reported marine debris removal activities | 5,560,328 | 7,342,283 | 5,214,067 |
| **Performance measure 10: Education and Training** | | | |
| Number of educational activities related to coastal habitat offered by state programs | 1,643 | 1,636 | 2,756 |
| Number of participants in educational activities related to coastal habitat offered by state programs | 110,244 | 77,059 | 94,464 |

| | 2011 | 2012 | 2013 |
|---|---|---|---|
| Number of training events related to coastal habitat offered by state programs | 95 | 120 | 867 |
| Number of participants in training events related to coastal habitat offered by state programs | 2,435 | 2,217 | 3,026 |

**Focus area: Coastal Hazards**

**Performance measure 11: Hazard Management**

| | 2011 | 2012 | 2013 |
|---|---|---|---|
| Number of communities that completed a project to reduce future damage from hazards with assistance from CZMP funding or state program staff | 150 | 47 | 68 |
| Number of communities that completed a project to increase public awareness of hazards with assistance from CZMP funding or state program staff | 25 | 57 | 47 |

**Performance measure 12: Education and Training**

| | 2011 | 2012 | 2013 |
|---|---|---|---|
| Number of educational activities related to coastal hazards offered by state programs | 180 | 225 | 296 |
| Number of participants in educational activities related to coastal hazards offered by state programs | 9,158 | 19,320 | 12,280 |
| Number of training events related to coastal hazards offered by state programs | 94 | 51 | 65 |
| Number of participants in training events related to coastal hazards offered by state programs | 2,769 | 3,147 | 1,934 |

**Focus area: Coastal Community Development**

**Performance measure 13: Sustainable Development and Waterfront Redevelopment**

| | 2011 | 2012 | 2013 |
|---|---|---|---|
| Number of coastal communities that developed or updated sustainable development ordinances, policies, and plans with assistance from CZMP funding or state program staff | 121 | 75 | 82 |
| Number of coastal communities that completed a project to implement a sustainable development plan with assistance from CZMP funding or state program staff | 15 | 9 | 17 |
| Number of coastal communities that developed or updated port or waterfront redevelopment ordinances, policies, and plans with assistance from CZMP funding or state program staff | 33 | 43 | 55 |
| Number of coastal communities that completed a project to implement a port or waterfront redevelopment plan with assistance from CZMP funding or state program staff | 7 | 10 | 6 |

| | 2011 | 2012 | 2013 |
|---|---|---|---|
| **Performance measure 14: Polluted Runoff Management** | | | |
| Number of coastal communities that developed or updated polluted runoff management ordinances, policies, and plans with assistance from CZMP funding or state program staff | 394 | 43 | 29 |
| Number of coastal communities that completed projects to implement polluted runoff management plans with assistance from CZMP funding or state program staff | 20 | 14 | 25 |
| **Performance measure 15: Education and Training** | | | |
| Number of educational activities related to coastal community development offered by state programs | 337 | 406 | 258 |
| Number of participants in educational activities related to coastal community development offered by state programs | 20,316 | 49,079 | 304,535 |
| Number of training events related to coastal community development offered by state programs | 104 | 69 | 96 |
| Number of participants in training events related to coastal community development offered by state programs | 3,118 | 1,802 | 2,277 |
| **Financial measures** | | | |
| **Performance measure 16: CZMP Federal and Matching Dollars Spent and Leveraged** | | | |
| Number of CZMP federal and matching dollars spent, by category: | | | |
| Number of dollars spent on government coordination | $29,329,142 | $30,171,489 | $33,469,124 |
| Number of dollars spent on public access | $10,725,475 | $10,041,236 | $11,117,341 |
| Number of dollars spent on coastal habitat | $16,004,722 | $15,564,484 | $18,393,891 |
| Number of dollars spent on coastal hazards | $9,253,705 | $9,744,802 | $8,324,826 |
| Number of dollars spent on coastal community development | $14,573,592 | $13,699,274 | $15,408,095 |
| Total number: | $79,886,635 | $79,221,285 | $86,713,278 |
| Number of dollars leveraged by CZMP funds, by category: | | | |
| Number of dollars leveraged for government coordination | $1,844,137 | $5,644,764 | $2,139,203 |
| Number of dollars leveraged for public access | $20,131,692 | $6,774,100 | $8,409,871 |
| Number of dollars leveraged for coastal habitat | $5,711,793 | $10,471,749 | $9,081,037 |
| Number of dollars leveraged for coastal hazards | $3,722,965 | $3,676,160 | $3,718,439 |
| Number of dollars leveraged for coastal community development | $6,268,895 | $10,916,677 | $4,924,452 |
| Total number: | $37,679,482 | $37,483,450 | $28,273,002 |

| | 2011 | 2012 | 2013 |
|---|---|---|---|
| **Performance measure 17: CZMP Federal and Matching Dollars Provided as Technical and Financial Assistance** | | | |
| Number of CZMP federal and matching dollars spent on technical assistance to local governments, by category: | | | |
| Number of dollars spent on technical assistance for government coordination | $5,983,609 | $5,204,857 | $6,220,180 |
| Number of dollars spent on technical assistance for public access | $1,558,676 | $1,567,885 | $2,145,533 |
| Number of dollars spent on technical assistance for coastal habitat | $3,356,390 | $1,938,202 | $3,165,608 |
| Number of dollars spent on technical assistance for coastal hazards | $2,039,983 | $1,705,382 | $1,651,832 |
| Number of dollars spent on technical assistance for coastal community development | $4,459,762 | $3,987,681 | $3,071,162 |
| Total number: | $17,398,420 | $14,404,007 | $16,254,314 |
| Number of CZMP federal and matching dollars provided as financial assistance to local governments, by category: | | | |
| Number of dollars provided as financial assistance for government coordination | $3,197,009 | $3,222,016 | $4,175,156 |
| Number of dollars provided as financial assistance for public access | $6,658,021 | $4,265,777 | $5,529,215 |
| Number of dollars provided as financial assistance for coastal habitat | $3,012,060 | $1,708,034 | $2,926,198 |
| Number of dollars provided as financial assistance for coastal hazards | $1,588,859 | $1,109,051 | $1,680,944 |
| Number of dollars provided as financial assistance for coastal community development | $4,455,786 | $5,659,039 | $6,587,395 |
| Total number: | $18,911,735 | $15,963,918 | $20,898,908 |

Source: GAO analysis of National Oceanic and Atmospheric Administration data. | GAO-14-592

Notes:

Focus areas and a financial measures category are highlighted in blue shading, corresponding performance measures are noted using dark gray shading, and supporting data elements that compose each performance measure are noted using light gray shading.

Measures data that involve acreages or dollar values may not add to the totals as listed due to rounding.

If a state program does not complete activities related to a given measure or data element during the reporting cycle, then it need not report data for that measure or element, according to a NOAA official. We found that the reported data for most measures and data elements do not contain data from all state programs. For example, in 2012, 33 states reported data on the total number of federal consistency projects reviewed, while 7 states reported data on the number of public access sites created through acquisition or easement with assistance from CZMP funding or state program staff.

CZMP performance measurement system data does not directly correspond to funds awarded to states each fiscal year. Because state programs have 3 years after funds are awarded to obligate CZMP funds before they must be returned to NOAA, performance measurement system data for a given fiscal year may include activities completed using funds awarded from up to 3 prior fiscal years.

[a]All state programs are required to report CZMP performance measurement system data to NOAA on an annual basis. NOAA officials indicated that states report data to the national performance measurement system as activities are completed. Specifically, states report data on a cycle that corresponds to the start date of their award (either July 1 or October 1) and reflect completed activities for the previous year (July 1 to June 30, or October 1 to September 30). For example, 2011 data represent activities completed between July 1, 2010 through June 30, 2011, or October 1, 2010 through September 30, 2011.

# Appendix III: Key Attributes of Successful Performance Measures Previously Identified by GAO

| Attributes | Definition | Potentially adverse consequences of not meeting attribute |
|---|---|---|
| Linkage | Measure is aligned with division and agency-wide goals and mission and clearly communicated throughout the organization. | Behaviors and incentives created by measures may not support achieving division or agency-wide goals or mission. |
| Clarity | Measure is clearly stated and the name and definition are consistent with the methodology used to calculate it. | Data may confuse or mislead users. |
| Numerical target | Measure has a numerical target. | Managers may not be able to determine whether performance is meeting expectations. |
| Objectivity | Measure is reasonably free from significant bias or manipulation. | Performance assessments may be systematically over- or understated. |
| Reliability | Measure produces the same result under similar conditions. | Reported performance data may be inconsistent and add uncertainty. |
| Core program activities | Measures cover the activities that an entity is expected to perform to support the intent of the program. | Information available to managers and stakeholders in core program areas may be insufficient. |
| Limited overlap | Measure provides new information beyond that provided by other data sources. | Manager may have to sort through redundant, costly information that does not add value. |
| Balance | Taken together, measures ensure that an organization's various priorities are covered. | Measures may over emphasize some goals and skew incentives. |
| Government-wide priorities | Each measure should cover a priority such as quality, timeliness, and cost of service. | A program's overall success is at risk if all priorities are not addressed. |

Sources: GAO, Environmental Justice: EPA Needs to Take Additional Actions to Help Ensure Effective Implementation, GAO-12-77 (Washington, D.C., Oct. 6, 2011) and Tax Administration: IRS Needs to Further Refine Its Tax Filing Season Performance Measures, GAO-03-143 (Washington, D.C.: Nov. 22, 2002). | GAO-14-592

# Appendix IV: Comments from the Department of Commerce

**THE DEPUTY SECRETARY OF COMMERCE**
Washington, D.C. 20230

June 25, 2014

Ms. Anne-Marie Fennell
Director
Natural Resources and Environment
U.S. Government Accountability Office
441 G Street NW
Washington, DC 20548

Dear Ms. Fennell:

Thank you for the opportunity to review and comment on the Government Accountability Office (GAO) draft report entitled *Coastal Zone Management: Opportunities Exist for NOAA to Enhance its Use of Performance Information* (GAO-14-592). Enclosed are the National Oceanic and Atmospheric Administration's programmatic comments to the draft report.

If you have any questions, please contact me or Margaret Cummisky, Assistant Secretary for Legislative and Intergovernmental Affairs at (202) 482-3663.

Sincerely,

Bruce H. Andrews
Acting Deputy Secretary of Commerce

Enclosure

**Department of Commerce**
**National Oceanic and Atmospheric Administration**
**Response to the GAO Draft Report Entitled**
**"Coastal Zone Management:  Opportunities Exist for NOAA to**
**Enhance its Use of Performance Information"**
**(GAO-14-592)**

<u>General Comments</u>

The Department of Commerce's National Oceanic and Atmospheric Administration (NOAA) appreciates the opportunity to review the Government Accountability Office's (GAO) draft report on the National Coastal Zone Management Program (CZMP).  This report does a good job characterizing this program, its efforts in responding to the 2008 GAO audit, and current performance measurement and evaluation efforts.  Also, the report is generally well informed and balanced.

The Coastal Zone Management Act (CZMA) establishes overarching goals and broad program requirements for states that choose to participate in the CZMP.  However, the Act also provides coastal states great flexibility in designing and administering coastal management programs that best meet a state's specific needs and authorities.  Therefore, each coastal management program is constructed differently and may focus on different CZMA goals which can make the establishment of national performance information that provides for informative national assessments, and yet recognizes the diversity and individuality of state coastal management programs, challenging at times.

As noted in the report, NOAA has already begun to look at ways to streamline and strengthen the CZMP performance measurement system to make it more effective and useful to the program.  The agency appreciates the thought GAO put into its examination of the CZMP's performance measurement system and other performance information and the resulting recommendations, which will help to shape future improvements.

While NOAA generally finds GAO's evaluation of the CZMP performance measurement system accurate, the agency does not agree with GAO's assessment that eliminating a stand-alone category for "coastal water quality" negatively affects the system's ability to reflect the goals of the CZMA in a balanced way (see discussion on page 21 of the report).  As the report notes, NOAA has retained a two-part measure to track the number of communities the CZMP works with to:  a) develop or update polluted runoff management ordinances, policies, and plans; and b) complete projects to implement polluted runoff management plans.  The fact that the remaining streamlined measure is no longer housed under a "coastal water quality" category heading but has been moved under the "coastal community development" category does not impair NOAA's ability to continue to track progress in meeting the water quality goal of the CZMA.

As the report notes, NOAA worked closely with the Coastal States Organization (CSO) to revise the water quality measures.  The NOAA/CSO workgroup recommended the coastal water quality performance measures be streamlined by deleting several measures and revising an additional measure.  The workgroup chose to streamline and consolidate the measures so that states could focus their time reporting on the most valuable measures related to the Act's broad water quality

1

goal. The workgroup recommended deleting measures that were less informative or too narrow in scope (e.g., the number of clean marinas). Many of these more specific activities could still be captured under part "b" of the existing performance measure if the activities were carried out to implement a broader polluted runoff management plan, which is often the case, especially for water quality monitoring.

The agency values the coastal water quality goal in the CZMA and recognizes that coastal water quality remains a priority for some coastal management programs. NOAA also recognizes the importance of having "balance" among its measures and will continue to consider that as it moves forward with its ongoing effort to improve the performance measurement system.

## NOAA Response to GAO Recommendations

The draft GAO report states, "To ensure that NOAA collects and uses meaningful performance information to help manage the CZMP, including continuing to improve its CZMP performance measurement system and its state program evaluations, we are recommending that the Secretary of Commerce direct the Administrator of NOAA to take the following three actions:"

**Recommendation 1**: "Develop a documented strategy to use the range of performance information the agency collects, as appropriate, to aid its management of the CZMP, such as to identify potential problems or weaknesses in the CZMP; set program priorities or strategies; or recognize and reward high-performing state programs."

**NOAA Response:** NOAA agrees with this recommendation. NOAA will develop a strategy to use the performance information it collects (performance measures, evaluations, performance reports, funding allocations, etc.) to support its management of the CZMP. In developing the strategy, NOAA will consider how the performance information can be used to help identify problems or weaknesses in the CZMP, set program and office priorities or strategies, communicate more effectively about the value of the program, and recognize and reward high-performing state programs. The strategy will also build upon existing efforts to share lessons-learned regarding successful approaches or shared challenges across the national program.

**Recommendation 2:** "As part of the intended review of the CZMP performance measurement system and in consideration of how it intends to use the performance information, document the approach it plans to take to analyze and revise, as appropriate, the performance measures, and in so doing ensure the analysis considers key attributes of successful performance measures, such as balance and limited overlap."

**NOAA Response:** NOAA agrees with this recommendation. The CZMP performance measurement system is considered an integral part of the ongoing analysis of performance measures across the newly integrated office. NOAA has staged the next phase of the specific CZMP performance measure analysis during FY 2015 so that it could be informed by and consistent with the GAO findings and recommendations. As the agency continues its process of developing and documenting its approach to analyze and revise, as appropriate, the performance measures, NOAA will examine how the CZMP measures and data communicate performance of the CZMP at a national level. NOAA will also look for opportunities to reference CZMP measures and data as a key element of overall office performance to inform program adjustment and ensure continued progress toward the implementation of the integrated office's strategic plan. NOAA anticipates that this may serve as an important additional factor when identifying

2

where to streamline within the current suite of measures, ensuring balance and limited overlap in accordance with GAO's key attributes of successful performance measures. In addition, NOAA will consider GAO's findings regarding areas of perceived overlap among existing performance reporting requirements.

**Recommendation 3:** "Revise the sampling methodology for selecting stakeholders to survey-- included as part of its state program evaluation process--to ensure perspectives are gathered from stakeholders representing a variety of program goals and are collected in an objective manner."

**NOAA Response:** NOAA agrees with this recommendation. We will revise the sampling methodology and pursue Paperwork Reduction Act clearance and approval for the revised methodology to ensure that stakeholders representing the variety of program goals are selected.

3

# Appendix V: GAO Contact and Staff Acknowledgments

| | |
|---|---|
| **GAO Contact** | Anne-Marie Fennell, (202)512-3841 or fennella@gao.gov |

| | |
|---|---|
| **Staff Acknowledgments** | In addition to the individual named above, Alyssa M. Hundrup (Assistant Director), Elizabeth Beardsley, Mark A. Braza, Elizabeth Curda, John Delicath, Tom James, Katherine Killebrew, Patricia Moye,  Dan Royer, Kiki Theodoropoulos, and Swati Sheladia Thomas made key contributions to this report. |

| | |
|---|---|
| **GAO's Mission** | The Government Accountability Office, the audit, evaluation, and investigative arm of Congress, exists to support Congress in meeting its constitutional responsibilities and to help improve the performance and accountability of the federal government for the American people. GAO examines the use of public funds; evaluates federal programs and policies; and provides analyses, recommendations, and other assistance to help Congress make informed oversight, policy, and funding decisions. GAO's commitment to good government is reflected in its core values of accountability, integrity, and reliability. |
| **Obtaining Copies of GAO Reports and Testimony** | The fastest and easiest way to obtain copies of GAO documents at no cost is through GAO's website (http://www.gao.gov). Each weekday afternoon, GAO posts on its website newly released reports, testimony, and correspondence. To have GAO e-mail you a list of newly posted products, go to http://www.gao.gov and select "E-mail Updates." |
| **Order by Phone** | The price of each GAO publication reflects GAO's actual cost of production and distribution and depends on the number of pages in the publication and whether the publication is printed in color or black and white. Pricing and ordering information is posted on GAO's website, http://www.gao.gov/ordering.htm. |
| | Place orders by calling (202) 512-6000, toll free (866) 801-7077, or TDD (202) 512-2537. |
| | Orders may be paid for using American Express, Discover Card, MasterCard, Visa, check, or money order. Call for additional information. |
| **Connect with GAO** | Connect with GAO on Facebook, Flickr, Twitter, and YouTube. Subscribe to our RSS Feeds or E-mail Updates. Listen to our Podcasts. Visit GAO on the web at www.gao.gov. |
| **To Report Fraud, Waste, and Abuse in Federal Programs** | Contact: <br><br> Website: http://www.gao.gov/fraudnet/fraudnet.htm <br> E-mail: fraudnet@gao.gov <br> Automated answering system: (800) 424-5454 or (202) 512-7470 |
| **Congressional Relations** | Katherine Siggerud, Managing Director, siggerudk@gao.gov, (202) 512-4400, U.S. Government Accountability Office, 441 G Street NW, Room 7125, Washington, DC 20548 |
| **Public Affairs** | Chuck Young, Managing Director, youngc1@gao.gov, (202) 512-4800 U.S. Government Accountability Office, 441 G Street NW, Room 7149 Washington, DC 20548 |

Please Print on Recycled Paper.